13,00

PERFECTIONISTS
& Other
Meticulous Types

CAREERS FOR

PERFECTIONISTS
& Other
Meticulous Types

Blythe Camenson

VGM Career Horizons
NTC/Contemporary Publishing Group

Library of Congress Cataloging-in-Publication Data

Camenson, Blythe.
    Careers for perfectionists & other meticulous types / Blythe Camenson.
      p. cm. — (Careers for you series)
    ISBN 0-8442-2061-2 (cloth). — ISBN 0-8442-2059-0 (pbk.)
    1. Vocational guidance. 2. Perfectionism (Personality trait)
  I. Title.   II. Title: Careers for perfectionists and other meticulous types.
  III. Series.
  HF5381.C2532   1999
  331.7′02—dc21   98–37298
                                                CIP

Published by VGM Career Horizons
A division of NTC/Contemporary Publishing Group, Inc.
4255 West Touhy Avenue, Lincolnwood (Chicago), Illinois 60646-1975 U.S.A.
Copyright © 1999 by NTC/Contemporary Publishing Group, Inc.
All rights reserved. No part of this book may be reproduced, stored in a retrieval
system, or transmitted in any form or by any means, electronic, mechanical,
photocopying, recording, or otherwise, without the prior permission of
NTC/Contemporary Publishing Group, Inc.
Printed in the United States of America
International Standard Book Number: 0-8442-2061-2 (cloth)
                                         0-8442-2059-0 (paper)

99 00 01 02 03 04 MV 17 16 15 14 13 12 11 10 9 8 7 6 5 4 3 2 1

To Jan Goldberg, a perfect friend and colleague,
and to Marshall J. Cook, a perfect gentleman

Contents

Acknowledgments

The author would like to thank the following perfectionists for providing information about their careers:

Peter Benton, Restoration Architect

Kent Brinkley, Landscape Architect

Susan Broadwater-Chen, Information Specialist/Freelancer Writer

Diane Camerlo, In-House Counsel

Lisa Eagleson-Roever, Engineer

Joan Gardner, Conservator

Sara Goodman, Attorney—Intellectual Property Specialist

Rod Stafford Hagwood, Fashion Editor

David Martin, Engineer

Nancy McVicar, Writer

Valarie Neiman, Academic Researcher

George T. Ragsdale, Attorney/Chemical Engineer

Moana Re, Management Analyst

Mary Tribble, Event Planner

Joel Witt, Actuary

CHAPTER ONE

Scrutinizing the Options

D o you cross every "t" and dot every "i"? Is your house as neat as a pin, your closets and drawers organized, a place for everything and everything in its place?

Although some people might call you fussy or a perfectionist, you know your special qualities are highly valued in a number of settings, particularly in the world of work.

Wouldn't you love a chance to get your ducks in a row—and get paid for it? *Careers for Perfectionists* will lead you toward careers that will allow you to put your talents to good use.

What Makes a Perfectionist

So many of the nouns and adjectives that describe a perfectionist carry negative connotations. After all, who would enjoy being called a nitpicker or a critical fusspot? But true perfectionists don't allow themselves to be rattled by silly labels. They know that their eye for detail and their need to solve exasperating problems have contributed to their success in the workplace.

Perhaps a fussbudget might not be as socially popular as the easygoing devil-may-care types, but whatever behaviors constitute a perfectionist's repertoire, on the job they are seen with a whole different set of nouns and adjectives: excellence, flawlessness, incomparability, and ideal.

Career Possibilities

Perfectionists possess qualities above and beyond an attention to detail. They are as diverse as are the areas of interests to explore. Some are thrilled by research or enjoy working with and manipulating numbers or words. Others find their niche working with the law, where contracts and other legal documents demand a perfectionist's touch. Still others might find satisfaction working with their hands as art restorers, surveyors, mapmakers, or architects.

The skills of the perfectionist may also translate well to the technical world, where careers in the many branches of engineering are waiting. Perfections are also great planners and apply their talents to pulling together impressive events—anything from weddings to corporate conferences. And, finally, who would make a better efficiency expert than a true perfectionist?

Although most employers expect a high performance level from employees, there are some careers where high performance just isn't enough. Perfection is very much necessary—and demanded. But that doesn't cause a problem for you, the career-oriented perfectionist. You strive for no less than perfection in everything you do.

This book will carefully examine the following careers that are ideal for perfectionists. If you put your thinking cap on, you can probably add scores of other options to the list.

Number Crunchers

You received the Best Math Student award in high school. You may go on to college and get a bachelor's degree in math or perhaps even an M.B.A. Statistics makes complete sense to you, and your school counselors are steering you toward a career as an actuary or an accountant. And that might just be the perfect choice for you. Meet an actuary in Chapter Two and learn about the life of an IRS accountant and decide for yourself.

Lawyers

F. Lee Bailey, Robert Shapiro, and Johnny Cocheran aside, Perry Mason is probably the best known lawyer in this country. His clients are always innocent, he always gets them off, and he always nabs the real criminal in the process.

But real life does not always follow the imagination of television writers. If you decide to pursue a career in criminal law, many of your clients will not be innocent, and you might not be able to get them all off. Some you'd even rather not represent. However, in our justice system, everyone is innocent until proven guilty and everyone is entitled to legal defense.

Criminal lawyers operate their own practices, work for private law firms, or represent clients under the auspices of the Public Defender's Office.

For every F. Lee Bailey, there's a Marcia Clark. For every Mason, a Burger. Lawyers who work for state attorneys general, prosecutors, and courts play a key role in the criminal justice system. At the federal level, attorneys investigate cases for the Department of Justice or other agencies. Also, lawyers at every government level help develop programs, draft laws, interpret legislation, establish enforcement procedures, and argue civil and criminal cases on behalf of the government.

But criminal trial work is not the only option open to lawyers. Just as doctors gear their careers toward a particular specialty, so do lawyers. Chapter Three will introduce you to a variety of law specializations—and they all require the talents of a perfectionist. Most of the work is detail oriented, some of it is frustrating, and some involves danger—but there's no greater reward than seeing justice at work.

Architects

Architects design buildings and other structures. Some also restore historic buildings or work with the landscape. Architects provide a wide variety of professional services to individuals and organizations planning a construction project. They may be involved in all phases of development, from the initial discussion of general ideas with the client through construction. Their duties require a number of detail-oriented skills, such as design, engineering, management, communication, and supervision.

Surveyors and Mapmakers

There are several groups of workers who measure and map the earth's surface including several categories of land surveyors, mapping scientists, and photogrammetrists. Each uses a variety of skills and tools to accomplish their painstaking tasks.

Surveyors and mapmakers work for architectural, engineering, and surveying firms. Many also work for federal, state, and local government agencies, including the Bureau of Land Management, the Army Corps of Engineers, the Forest Service, and highway departments and urban planning agencies.

Engineers

Engineers work to find economical solutions to practical technical problems. They design machinery, products, systems, and processes for the highest level performance attainable. In addition to their design work, they also develop products, test or maintain them—and even estimate the time and cost required to complete them.

Engineers work for a variety of firms, including engine companies, airplane manufacturers, and various agencies of federal, state, and local government.

Art Conservators

Nothing demands more painstaking accuracy than restoring a valuable piece of art. Restoration is often conceived of as trying to bring something back to its original condition. Sometimes, however, restoration work is intended to slow down further deterioration.

Art restorers (these days they are called art conservators) find work with museums, art galleries, and for private individuals. A large number are self-employed.

Researchers

Tracing a family tree, surfing the web for an obscure fact, helping a doctoral candidate find information to complete a dissertation are all research-based activities—and detail-oriented people willingly sink their teeth into such meaty projects.

Researchers can be found in almost any employment setting, from the hallowed halls of a university or library to a home office. Some have Ph.D.s; others are self-taught.

Writers and Editors

Writers, editors, and proofreaders all understand the meaning of the word *perfection*. Just as accountants are meticulous in the way they handle numbers, so are writers and related professionals when it comes to dealing with words.

Writing, revising, polishing, and searching for errors are all activities that require a strict attention to detail. A large number of employment settings are home to these word managers, including publishing companies and literary agencies, magazines, newspapers, and home-based freelance offices.

Event Planners

Can you imagine arranging a black tie, sit-down dinner for eight thousand NBA members and their friends and family? How about handling a budget of $50,000 or $100,000 or more for a big corporate party complete with lasers and fireworks? If you can imagine all that—and relish the idea—then a career as a special event planner might be just right for you.

Efficiency Experts

Improving the productivity and profitability of a business often falls into the capable hands of an efficiency expert. These detail-oriented professionals study the existing business practices and devise new plans for improving them. Some are employed by large corporations and work in-house; others work for consulting firms that deal with many different companies; still others are self-employed freelancers.

Choosing Your Field

People who perform exacting work give of themselves in many different capacities, providing a variety of valuable services. If you're reading this book, chances are you're already considering one of the many careers well suited to perfectionists.

But perhaps you'd like to know more about the working conditions the different fields offer or which area would best suit your personality, skills, and lifestyle. There are several factors to consider when deciding which sector to pursue. Each field carries with it different levels of responsibility and commitment. To identify occupations that will match your expectations, you need to know what each job entails.

Ask yourself the following questions and make note of your answers. Then, as you go through the following chapters, compare your requirements to the information provided by the professionals interviewed. Their comments will help you pinpoint the fields that interest you and eliminate those that would clearly be the wrong choice.

- How much time are you willing to commit to training? Some skills can be learned on the job or with a year or two of formal training; others can take considerably longer to learn.

- Do you want to work behind a desk, either at home or in a busy office, or would you prefer to be out and about, surveying property or supervising the construction of a building?

- Can you handle a certain amount of stress on the job, or would you prefer a quiet, work-alone environment?

- How much money do you expect to earn starting out and after you have a few years' experience under your belt? Salaries and earnings vary greatly in each chosen profession.

- How much independence do you require? Do you want to be your own boss or will you be content as a salaried employee?

- Can you pay attention to detail, handle paperwork, legal documents, technical specifications, and reports?

Knowing your expectations and then comparing them to the realities of the work will help you make informed choices.

Training

The training required for the various careers covered in this book vary greatly. Some positions are entry level, requiring no more than a high school education. Others demand that you be physically fit and have some prior work experience. Others require specific skills and from two to four years of college or a technical program. Still others require several years of post-graduate study after your bachelor's degree. In each chapter you will find the requirements for each field.

Salaries

Salaries vary widely from position to position. Factors such as the size of the company, the source of funding, or the region of the country can often determine salary levels more so than the complexity of the job or the level of the candidates' education and experience.

Some professional positions such as in engineering, law, or architecture can provide financial rewards that are quite hand-some; other jobs such as research or writing might come up at the lower end of the scale. How inventive you are and how willing you are to create your own opportunities can effect the size of your income.

For More Information

In Appendix A you will find professional associations for many of the career paths explored in this book. Most offer booklets and pamphlets with career information; some are free, but others might have a nominal charge. A phone call or letter will have information in the mail to you within a few days.

In Appendix B you will find a list of institutions offering training programs and internships in art conservation. Appendix C offers further resources for job hunting.

CHAPTER TWO

Number Crunchers

T here is probably no other field that demands perfection more than working with numbers. If you have a head for figures, you will find that there are all kinds of career opportunities available for dedicated number crunchers.

In this chapter, we cover three main areas of the number-crunching professions—accountants and auditors, actuaries, and statisticians—but the skills these professionals use translate easily to a number of additional fields.

Accountants and auditors design internal control systems and analyze financial data. Others for whom training in accounting is invaluable include appraisers, budget officers, loan officers, financial analysts and managers, bank officers, actuaries, underwriters, tax collectors and revenue agents, FBI special agents, securities sales workers, and purchasing agents.

Actuaries determine the probability of income or loss from various risk factors. Other workers whose jobs involve related skills include accountants, economists, financial analysts, mathematicians, rate analysts, rate engineers, risk managers, statisticians, and value engineers.

People in numerous occupations work with statistics. Among them are actuaries, mathematicians, operations research analysts, computer programmers, computer systems analysts, engineers, economists, financial analysts, information scientists, life scientists, mathematicians, operations research analysts, physical scientists, and social scientists.

Accountants and Auditors

Managers must have up-to-date financial information in order to make important decisions. Accountants and auditors prepare, analyze, and verify financial reports and taxes and monitor information systems that furnish this information to managers in all business, industrial, and government organizations.

The four major fields of accounting are public accounting, management accounting, government accounting, and internal auditing.

Public accountants have their own businesses or work for public accounting firms. They perform a broad range of accounting, auditing, tax, and consulting activities for their clients, who may be corporations, governments, nonprofit organizations, or individuals.

Management accountants (also called industrial, corporate, or private accountants) record and analyze the financial information of the companies for which they work.

Government accountants and auditors maintain and examine the records of government agencies and audit private businesses and individuals whose activities are subject to government regulations or taxation.

Internal auditors verify the accuracy of their organizations' records and check for mismanagement, waste, or fraud.

Within each field accountants often concentrate on one phase of accounting. For example, many public accountants concentrate on tax matters, such as preparing an individual's income tax returns and advising companies of the tax advantages and disadvantages of certain business decisions.

Others concentrate on consulting and offer advice on matters such as employee health care benefits and compensation, the design of companies' accounting and data processing systems, and controls to safeguard assets. Some specialize in forensic accounting, investigating and interpreting bankruptcies and other complex financial transactions.

Still others work primarily in auditing, examining a client's financial statements and reporting to investors and authorities that they have been prepared and reported correctly. However, fewer accounting firms are performing this type of work because of potential liability.

Management accountants analyze and interpret the financial information corporate executives need to make sound business decisions. They also prepare financial reports for nonmanagement groups, including stockholders, creditors, regulatory agencies, and tax authorities. Within accounting departments, they may work in financial analysis, planning and budgeting, cost accounting, and other areas.

Accountants and auditors also work for federal, state, and local governments. Government accountants see that revenues are received and expenditures are made in accordance with laws and regulations. Many persons with an accounting background work for the federal government as Internal Revenue Service agents or in financial management, financial institution examination, and budget analysis and administration.

Internal auditing is rapidly growing in importance. As computer systems make information more timely and available, top management can base its decisions on actual data rather than personal observation. Internal auditors examine and evaluate their firms' financial and information systems, management procedures, and internal controls to ensure that records are accurate and controls are adequate to protect against fraud and waste.

They also review company operations, evaluating their efficiency, effectiveness, and compliance with corporate policies and procedures, laws, and government regulations. There are many types of highly specialized auditors, such as electronic data processing auditors, environmental auditors, engineering auditors, legal auditors, insurance premium auditors, bank auditors, and health care auditors. In addition, a small number of trained accountants teach and conduct research at business and professional schools. Some work part time as accountants or consultants.

Tools

Computers are widely used in accounting and auditing. With the aid of special computer software packages, accountants summarize transactions in standard formats for financial records or organize data in special formats for financial analysis. These accounting packages are easily learned and require few specialized computer skills, greatly reducing the amount of tedious manual work associated with figures and records.

Personal and laptop computers enable accountants and auditors in all fields, even those who work independently, to use their clients' computer systems and to extract information from large mainframe computers.

Internal auditors may recommend controls for their organizations' computer systems to ensure the reliability of the systems and the integrity of the data. A growing number of accountants and auditors have extensive computer skills and specialize in correcting problems with software or developing software to meet unique data needs.

Working Conditions

Accountants and auditors work in offices, but public accountants frequently visit the offices of clients while conducting audits. Self-employed accountants may be able to do part of their work at home. Accountants and auditors employed by large firms and government agencies may travel to perform audits at clients' places of business, branches of their firms, or government facilities.

The majority of accountants and auditors generally work a standard forty-hour week, but many work longer, particularly if they are self-employed and free to take on the work of as many clients as they choose. For example, about four out of ten self-employed accountants and auditors work more than fifty hours per week, compared to one out of four wage and salary accountants and auditors. Tax specialists often work long hours during the tax season.

Job Outlook

Accountants and auditors held about 962,000 jobs in 1994. They worked in all types of firms and industries, but nearly one-third worked for accounting, auditing, and bookkeeping firms, or were self-employed.

The majority of accountants and auditors were unlicensed management accountants, internal auditors, or government accountants and auditors. However, in 1994 there were on record over five hundred thousand state-licensed Certified Public Accountants (CPAs), Public Accountants (PAs), Registered Public Accountants (RPAs), and Accounting Practitioners (APs).

Most accountants and auditors work in urban areas where public accounting firms and central or regional offices of businesses are concentrated. Roughly 10 percent of all accountants are self-employed, and less than 10 percent work part-time.

Some accountants and auditors teach full-time in junior colleges and colleges and universities; others teach part-time while working for private industry or government or as self-employed accountants.

Employment of accountants and auditors is expected to grow faster than the average for all occupations through the year 2005. Qualified accountants and auditors should have good job opportunities. Although the profession is characterized by a relatively low turnover rate, many openings will also arise as accountants and auditors retire, die, or move into other occupations because the field is so large.

CPAs should have the widest range of opportunities, especially as more states enact the 150-hour rule (see the section on Training and Qualifications for Accountants and Auditors later in this chapter) and it becomes more difficult to become a CPA.

As the economy grows, the number of business establishments will increase, requiring more accountants and auditors to set up their books, prepare their taxes, and provide management advice. As these businesses grow, the volume and complexity of information developed by accountants and auditors on costs, expenditures, and taxes will increase as well.

More complex requirements for accountants and auditors also arise from changes in legislation related to taxes, financial reporting standards, business investments, mergers, and other financial matters.

The changing role of public accountants, management accountants, and internal auditors will also spur job growth. Public accountants will perform less auditing work due to potential liability and less tax work due to growing competition from tax preparation firms, but they will assume an even greater management advisory role and expand their consulting services. These rapidly growing services will lead to increased demand for public accountants in the coming years.

Management accountants also will take on a greater advisory role as they develop more sophisticated and flexible accounting systems and focus more on analyzing operations rather than just providing financial data. Similarly, management will increasingly need internal auditors to develop new ways to discover and eliminate waste and fraud.

Despite growing opportunities for qualified accountants and auditors, competition for the most prestigious jobs such as those with major accounting and business firms will remain keen. Applicants with a master's degree in accounting, a master's degree in business administration with a concentration in accounting, or a broad base of computer experience will have an advantage.

Moreover, computers now perform many simple accounting functions, allowing accountants and auditors to incorporate and analyze more information. This increasingly complex work requires greater knowledge of more specialized areas, such as international business and current legislation, and expertise in specific industries.

Training and Qualifications

Most public accounting and business firms require applicants for accountant and internal auditor positions to have at least a bachelor's degree in accounting or a related field. Those wishing to pursue a bachelor's degree in accounting should carefully research accounting curricula before enrolling. Many states will soon require CPA candidates to complete 150 semester hours of coursework prior to taking the CPA exam, and many schools have altered their curricula accordingly.

Some employers prefer those with a master's degree in accounting or a master's degree in business administration with a concentration in accounting. Most employers also prefer applicants who are familiar with computers and their applications in accounting and internal auditing.

For beginning accounting and auditing positions in the federal government, four years of college (including twenty-four semester hours in accounting or auditing) or an equivalent combination of education and experience is required.

Previous experience in accounting or auditing can help an applicant get a job. Many colleges offer students an opportunity to gain experience through summer or part-time internship programs conducted by public accounting or business firms. Such training is invaluable in gaining permanent employment in the field.

Professional recognition through certification or licensure is also helpful. In most states CPAs are the only accountants who are licensed and regulated. Anyone working as a CPA must have a certificate and a license issued by a state board of accountancy. The vast majority of states require CPA candidates to be college graduates, but a few states substitute a certain number of years of public accounting experience for the educational requirement.

Based on recommendations made by the American Institute of Certified Public Accountants and the National Association of State Boards of Accountancy, some states currently require that CPA candidates complete 150 semester hours of college coursework, and many other states are working toward adopting this law. This 150-hour rule requires an additional thirty hours of coursework beyond the usual four-year bachelor's degree in accounting.

All states use the four-part Uniform CPA Examination prepared by the American Institute of Certified Public Accountants. The two-day CPA examination is rigorous, and only about one-quarter of those who take it each year pass each part they attempt. Candidates are not required to pass all four parts at once, although most states require candidates to pass at least two parts for partial credit. Many states require all sections of the test to be passed within a certain period of time. Most states also require applicants for a CPA certificate to have some accounting experience.

The designations PA or RPA are also recognized by most states, and several states continue to issue these licenses. With the growth in the number of CPAs, however, the majority of states are phasing out the PA, RPA, and other non-CPA designations by not issuing any more new licenses. Accountants who hold PA or RPA designations have similar legal rights, duties, and obligations as CPAs, but their qualifications for licensure are less stringent.

The designation Accounting Practitioner is also awarded by several states. It requires less formal training than a CPA license and covers a more limited scope of practice.

Nearly all states require both CPAs and PAs to complete a certain number of hours of continuing professional education before their licenses can be renewed. The professional associations representing accountants sponsor numerous courses, seminars, group study programs, and other forms of continuing education. (See Appendix A for a list of professional associations.)

Professional societies bestow other forms of credentials on a voluntary basis. Voluntary certification can attest to professional competence in a specialized field of accounting and auditing. It also can certify that a recognized level of professional competence has been achieved by accountants and auditors who acquired some skills on the job, without the level of formal education or public accounting work experience needed to meet the rigorous standards required to take the CPA examination. Increasingly, employers seek applicants with these credentials.

The Institute of Internal Auditors confers the designation Certified Internal Auditor (CIA) upon graduates from accredited colleges and universities who have completed two years' work in internal auditing and who have passed a four-part examination.

The EDP Auditors Association confers the designation Certified Information Systems Auditor (CISA) upon candidates who pass an examination and who have five years of experience in auditing electronic data processing systems. However, auditing or data processing experience and college education may be substituted for up to three years.

Other organizations, such as the National Association of Certified Fraud Examiners and the Bank Administration Institute, confer other specialized auditing designations.

The Institute of Management Accountants (IMA), formerly the National Association of Accountants, confers the Certified Management Accountant (CMA) designation upon college graduates who pass a four-part examination, agree to meet continuing education requirements, comply with standards of professional conduct, and have at least two years' work in management accounting. The CMA program is administered through an affiliate of the IMA, the Institute of Certified Management Accountants. The Accreditation Council for Accountancy and Taxation, a satellite organization of the National Society of Public Accountants, awards a Certificate of Accreditation in Accountancy to those who pass a comprehensive examination, and a Certificate of Accreditation in Taxation to those with appropriate experience and education. It is not uncommon for a practitioner to hold multiple licenses and designations. For instance, one internal auditor might be a CPA, CIA, and CISA.

If you are planning a career in accounting, you should have an aptitude for mathematics, be able to analyze, compare, and interpret facts and figures quickly, and make sound judgments based on this knowledge. Accountants and auditors must be able to clearly communicate the results of their work, orally and in writing, to clients and management.

Accountants and auditors must be good at working with people as well as with business systems and computers. Accuracy and the ability to handle responsibility with limited supervision are important. Perhaps most important, because millions of financial statement users rely on their services, accountants and auditors should have high standards of integrity.

Salaries

According to a National Association of Colleges and Employees survey in 1995, bachelor's degree candidates in accounting received starting salary offers averaging nearly $28,000 a year; master's degree candidates in accounting, $31,500.

According to another survey of workplaces in 160 metropolitan areas the most experienced accountants had median earnings of $77,200.

According to a survey conducted by Robert Half International, salaries of internal auditors in 1995 ranged from $23,000 for those with less than two years of experience to $84,500 for those with over ten years of experience.

In the federal government, the starting annual salary for junior accountants and auditors was about $18,700 in 1995. Candidates who had a superior academic record could begin at about $23,000. Applicants with a master's degree or two years' professional experience began at $28,300.

Accountants employed by the federal government in non-supervisory, supervisory, and managerial positions averaged $50,500 a year in 1995; auditors, $53,600.

What It's Really Like

Working for the IRS

The IRS is an agency of the Treasury Department of the United States. The national office is located in Washington, D.C. Under the national office are the regional offices, each covering several states. These offices oversee the various district offices located in each state. The number of district offices in each state differs depending on the population and the need of service to the population.

Each district office is divided into divisions, such as the Examination Division, the Collections Division, and the Criminal Investigation Division. Each division is then divided into branches, and each branch is made up of several groups. The group is the basic unit of the branch where the revenue agents, collection officers, or criminal investigation agents belong.

On-the-Job Training with the IRS

Once a person is hired as an Internal Revenue Agent, the IRS trains the new employee. The training consists of five phases, and each phase is divided into two types of training: classroom and on-the-job.

During the classroom training, the agents learn tax law and must take and pass tests. During the on-the-job training, the new agent conducts examinations under the guidance of an on-the-job instructor, who is usually an experienced agent. The total amount of time to complete these phases is about two to three years.

The first year working for the IRS is conditional. This means that if the agent does not pass the first couple of phases of training, he or she may be fired. After the first year, if the agent has passed all training during that year, the job becomes a career job or a permanent job.

What an IRS Audit Involves

An audit of a return, whether it is a return of an individual or an entity, is not just auditing the books and records of the person. An audit includes reviewing the financial status or economic reality of the person/entity. This means that the examiner (agent) must evaluate the facts and circumstances of each case to determine if what is reported on the return is credible or not. For example, if a company has been reporting losses for a few years, the agents wonder how the company manages to survive. Are there related entities that loan moneys to this company? Do the shareholders contribute more capital? Does the company get loans from financial institutions? If the answers to those questions are negative, then it is questionable that the company is in fact incurring losses every year.

Duties of an IRS Auditor

PLANNING OF WORK   Establish workload priorities for assigned cases, compliance activities (compliance means to ensure that all entities and people related to the cases the agents are assigned are in compliance with the tax laws, i.e., have filed tax returns), and other assignments, such as planning, scheduling and spending time on work-based priorities; planning the examinations, scheduling appointments required to conduct the examinations; and conducting examinations.

APPLICATION OF ACCOUNTING AND AUDITING PRINCIPLES Gain an understanding of the taxpayer's accounting practices and bookkeeping systems. Reconcile amounts on the returns to the books and records and analyze the relationship between the income statements and the balance sheets accounts in order to identify potential issues. Determine the quality of the internal control of the company through interviews with the people involved in the business, employees, and/or accountants. After assessing the control structure, select the audit techniques to use.

ISSUE IDENTIFICATION   Review the returns and internal control of the companies to determine which are the significant items that may have tax potential.

FACT FINDING   Gather adequate evidence to resolve the tax issues identified and support the conclusions reached. Evaluate the credibility of all evidence obtained.

APPLICATION OF TAX LAW   Conduct necessary research to understand and clarify the tax law applicable to the case issues and facts. Apply the Internal Revenue Code, regulations, rulings, court cases, etc., to the case facts to decide issues and arrive at the correct tax determination.

WRITTEN PRODUCT   Prepare work papers that reflect the audit steps taken and that support the conclusions reached. Prepare accurate examination reports, schedules, and forms. Assemble the case file to close the case.

CUSTOMER RELATIONS   Conduct contacts and discussions both inside and outside the IRS in a professional manner.

USE OF TIME   Try to consistently complete tasks so that the total time spent is relatively low, and the time span of activities is relatively short, considering the nature and complexity of the work.

Some Perks of the Job

The IRS allows its field employees (field employees are revenue agents, collections officers, CID agents, and anyone whose job requires that they go out of their offices in order to perform their duties) to work out of their home, if the employee so chooses. However, most field employees are expected to work in the field at least 50 to 80 percent of their time.

A revenue agent, for example, would have duties involving auditing corporations and partnerships, so his or her time would mostly be spent doing the examinations at the places of business or at the offices of the accountants that represent these entities.

A trip to the office is necessary only when there is a meeting, to do monthly reports, to pick up mail, to get cases, to submit cases, and to do research.

IRS employees may start work at any time between 7:00 and 9:00 A.M. and finish the day any time between 3:30 and 5:30 P.M. Employees may work part-time or accumulate compensatory time—work extra hours in order to use them when you need them later on.

In addition, agents do not have to take work home with them. This means that they work eight hours a day and the rest of the time is their own—contrary to accountants who work for private firms and who, at times, have to work overtime whether they want to or not.

Government employees accumulate a certain number of vacation and sick hours every pay period (each pay period is two weeks). As long as they have leave accumulated, they can take the hours any time they need them and in any increments (the lowest increment is one hour).

The Downsides

Working for the IRS often involves what seems like endless red tape, and advancement doesn't always come as quickly as you may wish. Agents also have to deal with the fact that they are working for and representing an entity that is disliked by most (if not all) people in this country.

Actuaries

Why do young drivers pay more for automobile insurance than older drivers? How much should an insurance policy cost? How much should an organization contribute each year to its pension fund? Answers to these and similar questions are provided by actuaries, who design insurance and pension plans and ensure that they are maintained on a sound financial basis.

Actuaries assemble and analyze statistics to calculate probabilities of death, sickness, injury, disability, unemployment, retirement, and property loss. They use this information to determine the expected insured loss. For example, they may calculate the probability of claims due to automobile accidents, which can vary depending on the insured's driving history, type of car, and many other factors.

They must make sure that the price charged for the insurance will enable the company to pay all claims and expenses as they occur. Finally, this price must be profitable and yet be competitive with other insurance companies.

In a similar manner, the actuary calculates premium rates and determines policy contract provisions for each type of insurance offered. Most actuaries specialize in either life, health, or property and casualty insurance; others specialize in pension plans or in financial planning and investment.

To perform their duties effectively, actuaries must keep informed about general economic and social trends and legislative, health, and other developments that may affect insurance practices. Because of their broad knowledge of insurance, company actuaries may work in investment, underwriting, or pension planning departments.

Actuaries in executive positions help determine company policy. In that role, they may be called upon to explain complex technical matters to other company executives, government officials, policyholders, and the public. They may testify before public agencies on proposed legislation affecting the insurance business, for example, or explain changes in premium rates or contract provisions. They also may help companies develop plans to enter new lines of business, such as environmental risk or long-term health care.

The small number of actuaries who work for the federal government usually deal with a particular insurance or pension program, such as Social Security or life insurance for veterans and members of the armed forces.

Actuaries in state government are usually employed by state insurance departments that regulate insurance companies, oversee the operations of state retirement or pension systems, handle unemployment insurance or workers' compensation problems, and assess the impact of proposed legislation. They might determine whether the rates charged by an insurance company are proper or whether an employee benefit plan is financially sound.

Consulting actuaries provide advice for a fee to various clients, including insurance companies, corporations, hospitals, labor unions, government agencies, and attorneys. Some consulting actuaries set up pension and welfare plans, calculate future benefits, and determine the amount of employer contributions. They also provide advice to health care and financial services firms.

Consultants may be called upon to testify in court regarding the value of potential lifetime earnings lost by a person who has been disabled or killed in an accident, the current value of future pension benefits in divorce cases, or the calculation of automobile insurance rates.

Actuaries who are enrolled under the provisions of the Employee Retirement Income Security Act of 1974 (ERISA) evaluate the pension plans covered by that act and report on their financial soundness.

Actuaries have desk jobs that require no unusual physical activity; their offices generally are comfortable and pleasant. They usually work at least forty hours a week. Some actuaries, particularly consulting actuaries, often travel to meet with clients. Consulting actuaries may also be expected to work more than forty hours per week.

Job Outlook

Actuaries held about seventeen thousand jobs in 1994. More than one in ten are self-employed. Well over one-half of wage and salary actuaries work in the insurance industry. Most work for life insurance companies; others work for property, casualty, and health insurance companies and insurance agents and brokers. Most of the remaining actuaries work for firms providing services, especially consulting actuarial services. A small number of actuaries work for government agencies.

Employment of actuaries is expected to grow faster than the average for all occupations through the year 2005. College graduates who have passed at least two actuarial examinations while still in school, have a strong mathematical and statistical background, have strong communication and problem-solving skills, and have gained some practical experience by completing an internship should have the best prospects.

Employment growth of consulting actuaries is expected to be faster than growth in life insurance companies, traditionally the major employer of actuaries. As companies seek to boost profitability by streamlining operations, some actuarial departments may be cut back or eliminated completely. Insurance companies may increasingly turn to consultants to provide actuarial services formerly performed in-house.

The need to assess the financial effects of prospective changes in the health care system and health problems, such as AIDS or heart disease, on insurance companies or government will result in continued overall employment growth.

Also, shifts in the age distribution of the population will result in a large increase in the number of people with established careers and family responsibilities. This is the group that traditionally has accounted for the bulk of private insurance sales. As people live and work longer, they draw health and pension benefits for a longer period, and actuaries are needed to re-estimate the probabilities of such events as death, sickness, and length of retirement.

The liability of companies for damage resulting from their products has received much attention in recent years. Casualty actuaries will continue to be involved in the development of product liability insurance, medical malpractice, workers' compensation coverage, and self-insurance, which may involve internal reserve funds established by some large corporations. The growing need to evaluate environmental risks and calculate prices for insuring facilities that carry such risks, such as underground storage tanks, will contribute to the demand for actuaries.

Despite expected employment growth, actuaries may face competition for jobs. Due to favorable publicity about the actuarial profession, the number of workers entering this small occupation has increased substantially in recent years, while at the same time, demand is expected to slow due to slower growth in the insurance industry.

Training and Qualifications

A good educational background for a beginning job in a large life or casualty company is a bachelor's degree in a mathematics- or business-related discipline, such as actuarial science, mathematics, statistics, economics, finance, or accounting. Some companies hire applicants with a liberal arts major, provided the applicant has a working knowledge of mathematics, including calculus, probability, and statistics, and has demonstrated this ability by passing at least the beginning actuarial exams required for professional designation. Courses in accounting, computer science, and insurance also are useful.

Companies increasingly prefer well-rounded individuals who, in addition to a strong technical background, have some training in liberal arts and business. Good communication and interpersonal skills are important, particularly for prospective consulting actuaries. Although only about fifty-five colleges and universities offer an actuarial science program, hundreds of schools offer a degree in mathematics or statistics.

A strong background in mathematics is essential for persons interested in a career as an actuary. It is an advantage to pass, while still in school, two or more of the examinations offered by professional actuarial societies. Three societies sponsor programs leading to full professional status in their specialty. The Society of Actuaries gives a series of actuarial examinations for the life and health insurance, pension, and finance and investment fields and the Casualty Actuarial Society gives a series of examinations for property and casualty issues. Because the first parts of the examination series of each society are jointly sponsored and cover the same material, students need not commit themselves to a specialty until they have taken the initial examinations.

These examinations test competence in subjects such as linear algebra, probability, calculus, statistics, risk theory, and actuarial mathematics. The first few examinations help students evaluate their potential as actuaries. Those who pass usually have better opportunities for employment and higher starting salaries.

Actuaries are encouraged to complete the entire series of examinations as soon as possible; completion generally takes from five to ten years. Examinations are given twice each year. Extensive home study is required to pass the advanced examinations; many actuaries study for several months to prepare for an examination. Actuaries who complete approximately half of the total examinations in either the life insurance series or the pension series, or seven examinations in the casualty series, are awarded associate membership in their society. Those who pass an entire series receive the title fellow.

The American Society of Pension Actuaries confers several designations, both actuarial and nonactuarial, for which requirements vary. However, membership status generally requires the passage of some actuarial exams as well as some pension experience.

Pension actuaries who attest to the federal government as to the financial status of defined benefit plans must be enrolled by the Joint Board for the Enrollment of Actuaries. Applicants for enrollment must meet certain experience, education, and examination requirements as stipulated by the Joint Board.

Beginning actuaries often rotate among jobs to learn various actuarial operations and different phases of insurance work, such as marketing, underwriting, or product development. At first, they prepare data for actuarial tables or perform other simple tasks. As they gain experience, they may supervise clerks, prepare correspondence and reports, and do research.

Salaries

In 1995, starting salaries for actuaries averaged about $36,000 for those with a bachelor's degree, according to the National Association of Colleges and Employers. New college graduates entering the actuarial field without having passed any actuarial exams averaged slightly lower salaries. Insurance companies and consulting firms give merit increases to actuaries as they gain experience and pass examinations. Some companies also offer cash bonuses for each exam passed.

A 1994 salary survey of insurance and financial services companies, conducted by the Life Office Management Association, Inc., indicated that actuarial students who have been designated Associate, Society of Actuaries, received an average salary of about $46,600. Newly designated Fellows in the Society of Actuaries received an average salary of nearly $72,700. Fellows with additional years of experience can earn substantially more.

Actuaries typically receive other benefits, including vacation and sick leave, health and life insurance, and pension plans.

What It's Really Like

Meet Joel Witt, Actuary

Joel Witt is an actuary with The National Council on Compensation Insurance, Inc. (NCCI), Residual Markets Division in Boca Raton, Florida. NCCI is the nation's largest information company serving the voluntary and involuntary workers' compensation and health care marketplaces.

Joel Witt earned his bachelor's degree in mathematics and statistics in 1992 from the University of Missouri, and his master's degree in statistics in 1994, also from the University of Missouri. He began working professionally after he graduated.

"I started at NCCI as a summer intern. I had obtained a copy of a directory that the Society of Actuaries (SOA) puts out that lists employers with such internship programs.

"I wanted to find a profession, other than teaching, that allowed me to utilize my mathematical skills. I also wanted to work in a business-oriented environment where I would interact with other people.

"Most actuaries either work in pricing or reserving departments of insurance companies. The pricing actuaries are the people that help determine how much an insured pays in premiums for an insurance policy.

"I work in reserving, which means that it is my responsibility to make sure that a company has adequately set reserves to fund future loss payments to claimants. NCCI is the administrator of many state workers' compensation residual market pools—the 'market of last resort' for employers who are unable to obtain voluntary workers' compensation coverage. These pools are risk-sharing mechanisms in which all insurers in a state are required to participate. It is my duty to predict how much loss will develop in these pools, so the participating insurance companies can adequately set reserves.

"Numbers are the lifeblood of an actuary's work. I spend much of my time analyzing historical data and gathering information about current and expected future trends that will impact an insurer. Frequently, I have to use computer applications to assist me in my analysis. I often have to make presentations to management and other actuaries, and, occasionally, I have to answer questions from other insurance companies, regulators, and auditors.

"The workload of an actuary varies by company. I normally work forty-hour weeks, but there are certain weeks every quarter that get hectic and require overtime.

"Most employers, including my own, offer a study program that allows their actuaries to take study time at work to prepare for their actuarial examinations.

"What I like most about my work is being involved in critical decisions that have a direct impact on the financial stability of a company. I also like interacting with other non-actuarial departments such as management, accounting, underwriting, and marketing.

"Actuaries must be aware of the quickly changing insurance environment both within a company and the whole insurance industry.

"The aspect I like least about the actuarial profession is the examination process. Passing the examinations is critical to professional advancement and necessary for membership in one of the actuarial societies. The examination process can seem overwhelming sometimes, requiring many study hours outside of work. Even the brightest actuarial candidate will need five to ten years to complete the entire series of examinations. Fortunately, most employers provide salary increases and/or promotions with each passed examination."

Advice from Joel Witt

"I would recommend getting a college degree in mathematics, statistics, or actuarial science if available. Some background in computers, finance, economics, and accounting is also helpful. This background will help a person get started on the actuarial exams. Most employers desire entry-level candidates to have passed at least the first two examinations. It also is important to have good communications skills.

"Many companies offer summer internship programs. This experience may help you decide if actuarial science is a career you want to pursue, and may lead to a full-time position after college.

"For the job hunt I would also recommend contacting the SOA and possibly the Casualty Actuarial Society (CAS). (Association addresses are listed in Appendix A.) I would also think that the Internet would be a good place to check for job postings.

Statisticians

Statistics is the collection, analysis, and presentation of numerical data. Statisticians design, implement, compile, and interpret the numerical results of surveys and experiments. In doing so, they often apply their knowledge of statistical methods to a particular subject area, such as biology, economics, engineering, medicine, or psychology. They may use statistical techniques to predict population growth or economic conditions, develop quality control tests for manufactured products, assess the nature of environmental problems, analyze legal and social problems, or help business managers and government officials make decisions and evaluate the results of new programs.

Often statisticians are able to obtain information about a group of people or things by surveying a small portion, called a sample, of the group. For example, to determine the size of the total audience for particular programs, television rating services ask only a few thousand families, rather than all viewers, which programs they watch. Statisticians decide where and how to gather the data, determine the type and size of the sample group, and develop the survey questionnaire or reporting form. They also prepare instructions for workers who will collect and tabulate the data. Statisticians use computers extensively to process large amounts of data for statistical modeling and graphic analysis.

Because statistics are used in so many areas, it is sometimes difficult to distinguish statisticians from specialists in other fields who use statistics. For example, a statistician working with data on economic conditions may have the title of economist.

Statisticians usually work regular hours in offices. Some statisticians may travel occasionally to supervise or set up a survey, or to gather statistical data. Some may do fairly repetitive tasks, while others may perform a variety of tasks, such as designing experiments.

Job Outlook

Statisticians held about fourteen thousand jobs in 1994. About one-fourth of these jobs were in the federal government, where statisticians were concentrated in the U.S. Departments of Commerce (especially the Bureau of the Census), Agriculture, and Health and Human Services. Most of the remaining jobs were in private industry, especially in the insurance, transportation equipment, research and testing services, management and public relations, and computer and data processing services industries. Others worked in colleges and universities and in business and professional organizations.

Although employment of statisticians is expected to grow more slowly than the average for all occupations through the year 2005, job opportunities should remain favorable. Many statistics majors, particularly at the bachelor's degree level, but also at the master's degree level, may find positions in which they do not have the title of statistician. This is especially true for those involved in analyzing and interpreting data from other disciplines such as economics, biological science, psychology, or engineering.

Among graduates with a bachelor's degree in statistics, those with a strong background in mathematics, engineering, or physical or computer science should have the best prospects of finding jobs related to their field of study in private industry or government.

Federal government agencies will need statisticians in fields such as agriculture, demography, consumer and producer surveys, transportation, Social Security, health, education, energy conservation, and environmental quality control. However, competition for entry-level positions in the federal government is expected to be strong for those just meeting the minimum qualification standards for statisticians.

Those who meet state certification requirements may become high school statistics teachers, a newly emerging field.

Private industry, in the face of increasing competition and strong government regulation, will continue to require statisticians, especially at the master's and Ph.D. degree levels, to not only monitor but improve productivity and quality in the manufacture of various products, including pharmaceuticals, motor vehicles, chemicals, and food products. For example, pharmaceutical firms will need more statisticians to assess the safety and effectiveness of the rapidly expanding number of drugs. To meet growing competition, motor vehicle manufacturers will need statisticians to monitor the quality of automobiles, trucks, and their components.

Statisticians with knowledge of engineering and the physical sciences will find jobs in research and development, working with scientists and engineers to help improve design and production processes in order to ensure consistent quality of newly developed products.

Business firms will rely more heavily than in the past on workers with a background in statistics to forecast sales, analyze business conditions, and help solve management problems.

In addition, sophisticated statistical services will increasingly be contracted out to consulting firms.

Training and Qualifications

A bachelor's degree with a major in statistics or mathematics is the minimum educational requirement for many beginning jobs in statistics. The training required for employment as an entry-level statistician in the federal government is a college degree including at least fifteen semester hours of statistics or a combination of fifteen hours of mathematics and statistics if at least six semester hours are in statistics. An additional nine semester hours in another academic discipline, such as economics, physical or biological science, medicine, education, engineering, or social science, are also required. To qualify as a mathematical statistician in the federal government requires twenty-four semester hours of mathematics and statistics, with a minimum of six semester hours in statistics and twelve semester hours in mathematics at the calculus level or higher.

Teaching and research positions in institutions of higher education and many positions in private industry require a graduate degree, often a doctorate, in statistics.

About eighty colleges and universities offered bachelor's degrees in statistics in 1994. Many other schools also offered degrees in mathematics, operations research, and other fields that included a sufficient number of courses in statistics to qualify graduates for some beginning positions, particularly in the federal government. Required subjects for statistics majors include mathematics through differential and integral calculus, statistical methods, mathematical modeling, and probability theory.

Additional courses that undergraduates should take include linear algebra, design and analysis of experiments, applied multivariate analysis, and mathematical statistics. Because computers are used extensively for statistical applications, a strong background in computer science is highly recommended.

For positions involving quality and productivity improvement, training in engineering or physical science is useful. A background in biological or health science is important for positions involving the preparation and testing of pharmaceutical or agricultural products. For many jobs in market research, business analysis, and forecasting, courses in economics and business administration are helpful.

In 1994, approximately 110 universities offered a master's degree program in statistics, and about 70 had statistics departments that offered a doctoral degree program. Many other schools also offered graduate level courses in applied statistics for students majoring in biology, business, economics, education, engineering, psychology, and other fields.

Acceptance into graduate statistics programs does not require an undergraduate degree in statistics, although a good mathematics background is essential.

Good communications skills are important for prospective statisticians, not only for those who plan to teach, but also to qualify for many positions in industry, where the need to explain statistical processes to nonstatisticians is common. A solid understanding of business and management is also important for those who plan to work in private industry.

Beginning statisticians who have only the bachelor's degree often spend much of their time doing routine work supervised by an experienced statistician. With experience, they may advance to positions of greater technical and supervisory responsibility. However, opportunities for promotion are best for those with advanced degrees. Master's and Ph.D. degree holders enjoy greater independence in their work and are qualified to engage in research, to develop statistical methodology, or, after several years of experience in a particular area of technological application, to become statistical consultants.

Salaries

The average annual salary for statisticians in the federal government in nonsupervisory, supervisory, and managerial positions was $56,899 in 1995; mathematical statisticians averaged

$60,510. Statisticians who hold advanced degrees and work in private industry generally earn higher starting salaries than their counterparts in academic settings and in government.

Benefits for statisticians tend to resemble those offered most professionals who work in an office setting: vacation and sick leave, health and life insurance, and a retirement plan, among others.

CHAPTER THREE

Lawyers

T he more detailed aspects of a lawyer's job depend upon his or her field of specialization and position. Even though all lawyers are allowed to represent parties in court, some appear in court more frequently than others. Lawyers who specialize in trial work must possess the ability to think quickly, be able to speak with ease and authority, and be thoroughly familiar with courtroom rules and strategy. Trial lawyers still spend most of their time outside the courtroom conducting research, interviewing clients and witnesses, and handling other details in preparation for trial.

Areas of Specialty

Besides trials, lawyers may specialize in other areas. The majority of lawyers are in private practice where they may concentrate on criminal or civil law.

Criminal Lawyers

In criminal law, lawyers represent individuals who have been charged with crimes and argue their cases in courts of law.

Civil Lawyers

In civil law, attorneys assist clients with litigation, wills, trusts, contracts, mortgages, titles, and leases. Some manage property as trustee or, as executor, see that provisions of a client's will are carried out. Others handle only public interest cases, civil or criminal, that have a potential impact extending well beyond the individual client. Other lawyers work for legal aid societies, which are private, nonprofit organizations established to serve disadvantaged people. These lawyers generally handle civil rather than criminal cases. Some other specializations within civil law include:

bankruptcy

probate

international law

environmental law

intellectual property

insurance law

family law

real estate law

public defense

House Counsel

Lawyers sometimes are employed full-time by a single client. If the client is a corporation, the lawyer is known as house counsel and usually advises the company about legal questions that arise from its business activities. These questions might involve patents, government regulations, contracts with other companies, property interests, or collective bargaining agreements with unions.

Government Attorneys

Attorneys employed at the various levels of government make up still another category. Lawyers working for state attorneys general, prosecutors, public defenders, and courts play a key role in the criminal justice system. At the federal level, attorneys investigate cases for the Department of Justice or other agencies. Also, lawyers at every government level help develop programs, draft laws, interpret legislation, establish enforcement procedures, and argue civil and criminal cases on behalf of the government.

Law Clerks

Law clerks are fully trained attorneys who choose to work with a judge, either for a one- to two-year stint out of law school or as a full-time, professional career. Their duties involve mainly research and writing reports.

Law Professors

A relatively small number of trained attorneys work in law schools. Most are faculty members who specialize in one or more subjects, and others serve as administrators. Some work full-time in nonacademic settings and teach part-time.

Working Conditions

Lawyers and judges do most of their work in offices, law libraries, and courtrooms. Lawyers sometimes meet in clients' homes or places of business and, when necessary, in hospitals or prisons. They frequently travel to attend meetings, to gather evidence, and to appear before courts, legislative bodies, and other authorities.

Salaried lawyers in government and private corporations generally have structured work schedules. Lawyers in private practice may work irregular hours while conducting research, conferring with clients, or preparing briefs during nonoffice hours.

Lawyers often work long hours, and about half regularly work fifty hours or more per week. They are under particularly heavy pressure, for example, when a case is being tried. Preparation for court includes keeping abreast of the latest laws and judicial decisions.

Although work generally is not seasonal, the work of tax lawyers and other specialists may be an exception. Because lawyers in private practice can often determine their own workload and when they will retire, many stay in practice well beyond the usual retirement age.

No matter the setting, whether acting as advocate or prosecutor, all attorneys interpret the law and apply it to specific situations. This requires research and communication abilities.

Lawyers perform in-depth research into the purposes behind the applicable laws and into judicial decisions that have been applied under circumstances similar to those currently faced by the client. While all lawyers continue to make use of law libraries to prepare cases, some supplement their search of the conventional printed sources with computer software packages that automatically search the legal literature and identify legal texts that may be relevant to a specific subject.

In litigation that involves many supporting documents, lawyers may also use computers to organize and index the material. They then communicate to others the information obtained by research.

What It's Really Like

Meet George Ragsdale,
Attorney/Chemical Engineer

George Ragsdale wears several hats—and they all require him to keep his eye to the details of his work. He is currently a vice president at Simons Engineering, Inc., an engineering/design firm located in Atlanta, Georgia. He graduated from Cornell University in 1973 with a B.S. in chemical engineering. He later received a J.D. degree from Widener University in 1992 and an M.B.A. from Widener in 1993.

George Ragsdale's Background

"I started working in the engineering field immediately upon graduation from Cornell in 1973 and began the practice of law immediately upon passing the Pennsylvania Bar in 1992.

"I wanted to be a chemical engineer from the time I was in about fourth grade. I always loved chemistry and math as a child and thought that the chemical engineering field would be very challenging and interesting to me.

"Later, as my roles shifted from actually performing engineering projects to managing an engineering department, I found myself not as fulfilled as when I first began engineering work. Plus, I had always had a love for the law and a lot of people, primarily my wife, encouraged me to go to law school. After graduating from law school, I continued to manage an engineering department full-time and began a family law practice on a part-time basis. Then, an opportunity arose to combine both my legal training and my engineering background and I jumped at the chance.

"One of the things I really enjoy about my current role is that every day is different and unpredictable. Every day is a mixture of reviewing project performance, reviewing client contracts, and a lot of other things. Aside from being general counsel for our firm, I also manage the accounting, finance, and human resources functions. Each of these disciplines has its own unique challenges that are collectively guaranteed to keep each day interesting.

"I consider the real upside of my job to be the opportunity to continue to learn while working at something I enjoy. Because my legal training and experience was quite narrow when I began this job, there are a lot of opportunities for me to become proficient in other areas of the law and rely less on outside counsel for assistance. The downside is that I personally have a tendency to try to do it all. And, on occasion, I overcommit because I really love what I am doing—almost too much!

Advice from George Ragsdale

"For anyone who has similar interests to mine—both law and engineering—I recommend some practical experience in the engineering field first. I would also advise that in whatever field you may want to practice law, firsthand experience with the operation of that field of work provides a tremendous advantage in the legal profession over others who may not have had that practical experience."

To learn about other careers in engineering, turn to Chapter Eleven.

Meet Sara Goodman, Intellectual Property Specialist

Sara Goodman is a solo practitioner, concentrating in intellectual property law, publishing matters, contracts, copyright, libel, and defamation. She received her B.A. with honors in history from Rice University in Houston, Texas, in 1978 and her J.D. with honors from New York University School of Law in New York City in 1982. She is a member of the New York and Florida Bars.

Sara Goodman's Background

"I decided to go to law school because, as corny or nostalgic as it may seem, my father had, from as long as I can remember, always told everyone that I was going to go to law school and follow in his footsteps. He was a unique and, perhaps in some ways, an anachronistic lawyer—a solo practitioner with a lot of sophisticated appellate work in a small city. He was educated at Harvard Law School in the 1930s, interested in helping his clients solve personal and professional problems and, more often than not,

not billing them for his services. This has become a repeated theme in my own life!

"When I was very young, in the early 1960s, he argued a case before the U.S. Supreme Court—my whole family went down to hear the argument—and I remember being in awe of the pomp and ceremony at the Court, of the respect given to the law and to the justices and to the entire court system. Interestingly, his opponent, who won the case, was a woman attorney working for the New York Attorney General's office, and my father went out of his way to impress on me the fact that being a girl would in no way stop me from being a successful lawyer. He also had two to three woman lawyers clerking for him over the years, and while these facts might seem insignificant now, they were not insignificant in the 1960s and early 1970s when female attorneys were still very few and very far between, particularly in small cities.

"I worked in his office during summers when I was about twelve to fifteen, acting as a general office gopher and helper, and I was always introduced to people as his youngest child, the one who was going to go to law school.

"In my senior year of college, my father learned he had liver cancer and had only a few months to live. He wanted me to go to law school so badly. I remember him telling me just a few weeks before he died about some of the schools he thought I should consider.

"In the end, I think the decision was influenced a lot by my emotions at the time, as well as an inability at that time in my life—I was only twenty-one—to figure out how to pursue other interests that I had. Also, everyone I knew said something to the effect that going to law school would always be helpful 'no matter what else you decided to do.' I don't know any lawyer who wasn't told the same thing."

On the Job

"When I was at Sullivan & Cromwell, a huge Wall Street firm with more than two hundred lawyers worldwide, the atmosphere was more formal and hierarchical, although I think S&C was more laid back than some firms of its kind. I spent huge numbers of hours in the law library doing lots of legal research and drafting memos and briefs in cases for huge corporate clients mostly. I also spent a lot of time doing 'discovery' and 'motion practice' in big litigation matters—which meant I spent a lot of time reviewing reams of documents and deciding which ones had to be turned over to our adversaries.

"At Simon & Schuster and Bantam Doubleday Dell, my in-house work was totally different than at S&C. I was on the 'front line' with my clients, helping them make practical decisions all day long and anticipating legal problems that I was able to help them avoid through careful planning. I worked on a lot of contracts and manuscripts. I also really liked working on books—they're probably the nicest type of product I can think of working with, as opposed to something like widgets or soap or toilet paper—not that we don't need widgets, soap, and toilet paper!

"I worked with a lot of interesting authors—some of whom were really wonderful and some of whom were kind of a pain in the neck.

"Now, in my own practice, which I would characterize as a 'part-time' practice at this point in time, I do a lot of the same things that I did in-house because I usually prefer to stay away from litigation matters, referring them to others, and taking things on that, for the most part, help people avoid legal problems with others.

"I represent writers and publishers who want help with their publishing contracts or their collaboration or work-for-hire agreements. I help authors plan ahead of time if they are taking on a project that will necessarily raise lots of legal flags.

"I sometimes represent my former employer, Bantam Doubleday Dell, on a freelance basis, helping their legal department with their overflow of manuscript reviews. This means that I read a book before it gets published and work with the author and editor to help ensure that the publisher and author do not get any successful legal claims against them on publication—e.g., claims for libel, invasion of privacy, and copyright infringement mostly.

"I like the area of law that I practice in a lot. Unlike most attorneys I know, I honestly think that the law—at least intellectual property law—is interesting. I also like helping people solve problems in connection with something that matters to them.

"What I like least is the billing of clients. I hate keeping track of my time and I can never bill clients for all of my time. I just want to do a really good job for people even if it takes a lot of time that I won't charge the client for. I really disliked this aspect of lawyering when I was an associate in a large law firm."

Advice from Sara Goodman

"Make sure you're burning up with love for the practice of law before going to law school because law is not an easy profession to be in these days. Even though I really liked law school and actually like what I do, many lawyers dislike law school and eventually leave the practice of law. In fact, most law students have no notion about what they really want to do with their law degree. So, unfortunately, young lawyers will find a lot of unhappiness and burnout among their colleagues. I think this is more common among litigators because the judicial system is often a frustrating arena in which to solve problems for clients.

"The litigation system is mind boggling to most laypeople—it's extremely expensive, it's extremely time consuming, we have so few really outstanding judges, and, unfortunately, the really frivolous cases give many good lawyers an undeserved bad reputation.

"Certainly anyone who is happy and content with his current career should not seek out a law degree simply to improve his economic standing—it's a circuitous and very unsteady path.

"I think the most important qualities you need to be a good lawyer are integrity and compassion—and it also definitely helps to be an excellent writer."

Meet Diane Camerlo, In-House Counsel

Diane Camerlo works with four other lawyers in the legal department of the Federal Reserve Bank of St. Louis. She received her B.A. from Denison University in Granville, Ohio, with a double major in sociology and English. In 1976, she earned her J.D. from Franklin Pierce Law Center in Concord, New Hampshire. She has been practicing for more than twenty years.

Diane Camerlo's Background

"When I graduated from college with a B.A. in sociology and English, I realized my career choices were limited to low-level jobs that would only lead to careers that didn't interest me. I considered various graduate school options and chose law because I believed lawyers did interesting, challenging work and were well paid and highly respected. My father had practiced law before taking a business position, so the field was familiar to me.

"In 1976 I began working as an associate in a law firm in Toledo, Ohio, and then later became a partner. The firm had about thirty-five to forty-five lawyers. I practiced mostly antitrust law, including complex litigation, but when Reagan dried up antitrust I did workers' comp. That was the pits after antitrust, so later I quit and moved to Rochester, New York, and sold computers until my daughter was born. I then took a law/business/computer job with a former legal client (a bank) and then I took a job in the Monsanto corporate legal department doing antitrust and general corporate work. I was only a contractor in that job (i.e. no benefits) so when the Fed job opened up, I took it. Thus, I've had experience in just about every way a lawyer can have experience except as a prosecutor, public defender, or judge."

On the Job

"The Federal Reserve Bank of St. Louis is one of the twelve operating arms of the Federal Reserve System located throughout the nation that together with their twenty-five branches carry out various system functions, including operating a nationwide payments system, distributing the nation's currency and coin, supervising and regulating member banks and bank holding companies, and serving as banker for the U.S. Treasury.

"My day is usually made up of some combination of meetings, client counseling, research, writing, planning, public speaking, telephone calls, traveling, and administrative duties. I could spend an entire day doing any one of those things, or I could do all of those things during the course of the day. I also attend continuing legal education seminars from time to time and serve on business-related committees and task forces.

"In my law department the lawyers don't have rigidly defined areas of specialization, so each of us works on a wide variety of projects. The areas of law that might be involved include: employment, employee benefits, contract, commercial, intellectual property, banking, general corporate, antitrust, environmental, safety, technology, tax, litigation, or just about anything else. Most of my work involves contracts, employment, banking or technology law. I also review bank holding company applications required to be filed with the Federal Reserve. We also monitor pending federal and state legislation that affects our industry.

"I am usually very busy with twenty or more active projects going on at one time. During the week I work nine to ten hours on a typical day, though I sometimes work a much longer (or occasionally shorter) day.

"The atmosphere in my law department is businesslike and friendly. The lawyers usually work on individual projects, but we frequently confer with each other. This give and take between attorneys enables us to provide better legal advice to our clients and also makes the job more rewarding.

"I like the intellectual challenge and stimulation of practicing law. I like working in a corporation where I can understand the business in depth and work with the business people to achieve the corporation's goals. I also enjoy the supportive atmosphere in our legal department.

"The primary downside to practicing law is the high level of pressure. Lawyers must give accurate legal advice, often with very short time limits. Another downside is the confrontational nature of the legal practice. Fortunately, this is much less a factor in an in-house corporate practice than in a law firm practice. Finally, the low opinion of lawyers by the general public is sometimes hard to take. While there are some bad apples in the legal profession, as in all professions, in my law department we place a high value on ethical behavior and client service."

Advice from Diane Camerlo

"For anyone considering a career in law I would recommend going to the best law school possible and getting the highest grades possible. Grades are especially important. The market for new lawyers is tight and those with low grades will have more trouble getting a job than those with high grades."

Training and Qualifications

To practice law in the courts of any state or other jurisdiction, a person must be licensed, or admitted to its bar, under rules established by the jurisdiction's highest court. Nearly all require that applicants for admission to the bar pass a written bar examination. Most jurisdictions also require applicants to pass a separate written ethics examination. Lawyers who have been admitted to the bar in one jurisdiction occasionally may be admitted to the bar in another without taking an examination if they meet that jurisdiction's standards of good moral character and have a specified period of legal experience. Federal courts and agencies set their own qualifications for those practicing before them.

To qualify for the bar examination in most states, an applicant must complete at least three years of college and graduate from a law school approved by the American Bar Association (ABA) or the proper state authorities. (ABA approval signifies that the law school, particularly its library and faculty, meets certain standards developed by the Association to promote quality legal education.)

Seven states accept the study of law in a law office or in combination with study in a law school; only California accepts the study of law by correspondence as qualifying for taking the bar examination.

Several states require registration and approval of students by the State Board of Law Examiners, either before they enter law school or during the early years of legal study.

The required college and law school education usually takes seven years of full-time study after high school: four years of undergraduate study, followed by three years in law school. Although some law schools accept a very small number of students after three years of college, most require applicants to have a bachelor's degree. To meet the needs of students who can attend only part-time, a number of law schools have night or part-time divisions which usually require four years of study.

Acceptance by most law schools depends on the applicant's ability to demonstrate an aptitude for the study of law, usually through good undergraduate grades, the Law School Admission Test (LSAT), the quality of the applicant's undergraduate school, any prior work experience, and sometimes a personal interview. However, law schools vary in the weight they place on each of these factors.

All law schools approved by the American Bar Association require that applicants take the LSAT. Nearly all law schools require that applicants have certified transcripts sent to the Law School Data Assembly Service. This service then sends applicants' LSAT scores and their standardized records of college grades to the law schools of their choice. Both this service and the LSAT are administered by the Law School Admission Services.

Graduates receive the degree of juris doctor (J.D.) or bachelor of law (LL.B.) as the first professional degree. Advanced law degrees may be desirable for those planning to specialize, do research, or teach. Some law students pursue joint degree programs, which generally require an additional year. Joint degree programs are offered in a number of areas, including law and business administration and law and public administration.

Salaries

Contrary to the experience of John Grisham's hero in *The Firm*, annual salaries of beginning lawyers in private industry average about $36,600. But top graduates from the nation's best law schools can start in some cases at over $80,000 a year. In the federal government, annual starting salaries for attorneys in ranges from about $28,000 to $35,000, depending upon academic and personal qualifications. Other factors affecting the salaries offered to new graduates include: academic record; type, size, and location of employer; and the specialized educational background desired.

Salaries of experienced attorneys also vary widely according to the type, size, and location of their employer. The average salary of the most experienced lawyers in private industry runs about $134,000, but some senior lawyers who are partners in the nation's top law firms can earn over $1 million. General attorneys in the federal government averaged around $65,000 a year in 1996.

Lawyers on salary receive increases as they assume greater responsibility. Lawyers starting their own practice may need to work part-time in other occupations during the early years to supplement their incomes. Their incomes usually grow as their practices develop. Lawyers who are partners in law firms generally earn more than those who practice alone.

Architects

T he design of a building involves far more than its appearance. Buildings must also be functional, safe, and economical and must suit the needs of the people who use them. Architects take all these things into consideration when they design buildings and other structures.

The architect and client first discuss the purposes, requirements, and budget of a project. Based on the discussions, the architect may prepare a report specifying the design requirements. In some cases, the architect assists in conducting feasibility and environmental impact analyses and selecting a site. The architect then prepares drawings and written information presenting ideas for the client to review.

After the initial proposals are discussed and accepted, the architect develops final construction plans. These plans show the building's appearance and details for its construction. Accompanying these are drawings of the structural system; air-conditioning, heating, and ventilating systems; electrical systems; plumbing systems; and possibly site and landscape plans.

Architects also specify the building materials and, in some cases, the interior furnishings. In developing designs, architects follow building codes, zoning laws, fire regulations, and other ordinances, such as those that require easy access by disabled persons. Throughout the planning stage, the architect makes necessary changes.

While architects have traditionally used pencil and paper to produce design and construction drawings, architects are increasingly turning to computer-aided design and drafting (CADD) technology for these important tasks.

The architect may also assist the client in obtaining construction bids, selecting a contractor, and negotiating the construction contract. As construction proceeds, the architect may be employed by the client to visit the building site in order to ensure that the contractor is following the design, meeting the schedule, using the specified materials, and meeting the specified standards for the quality of work. The job is not complete until all construction is finished, required tests are made, and construction costs are paid.

Architects design a wide variety of buildings, such as office and apartment buildings, schools, churches, factories, hospitals, houses, and airport terminals. They also design multibuilding complexes such as urban centers, college campuses, industrial parks, and entire communities. In addition to designing buildings, architects may advise on the selection of building sites, prepare cost analysis and land-use studies, and do long-range planning for land development.

Specializations

Architects sometimes specialize in one phase of work. Some specialize in the design of one type of building, such as hospitals, schools, or housing. Others specialize in construction management or the management of their firm and do little design work.

Historical architecture, or restoration architecture as it is also called, involves the meticulous work of returning a building to its former appearance at a particular period in history.

Landscape architecture is the design of outside areas that are beautiful, functional, and compatible with the natural environment. A landscape architect can work with small residential or commercial projects, or with complex projects on a much larger scale. These could include projects for cities or counties, industrial parks, historical sites, and a variety of other settings.

Working Conditions

Architects generally work in a comfortable environment. Most of their time is spent in offices advising clients, developing reports and drawings, and working with other architects and engineers. However, they also often work at construction sites reviewing the progress of projects.

While a forty-hour workweek is usual, architects may occasionally be under great stress, working nights and weekends to meet deadlines.

Training and Qualifications

All states and the District of Columbia require individuals to be licensed (registered) before they may call themselves architects or contract to provide architectural services. Many architecture school graduates work in the field even though they are not licensed. However, a licensed architect is required to take legal responsibility for all work.

Three requirements generally must be met for licensure:

- a professional degree in architecture

- a period of practical training or internship (usually for three years)

- passage of all sections of the Architect Registration Examination

In most states, the professional degree must be from one of the approximately one hundred schools of architecture with programs accredited by the National Architectural Accrediting Board. There are several types of professional degrees in architecture. Over half of all architecture degrees are from five-year bachelor of architecture programs intended for students entering from high school. Some schools offer a two-year master of architecture program for students with a preprofessional undergraduate degree in architecture or a related area, or a three- or four-year master of architecture program for students with a degree in another discipline. In addition, there are many combinations and variations of these degree programs.

The choice of degree type depends upon each individual's preference and educational background. Prospective architecture students should carefully consider the available options before committing to a program. For example, although the five-year bachelor of architecture program offers the fastest route to the professional degree, courses are specialized and, if the student does not complete the program, moving to a nonarchitecture program may be difficult.

A typical program includes courses in architectural history and theory, building design—including its technical and legal aspects—professional practice, math, physical sciences, and liberal arts. Many architecture schools also offer graduate education for those who already have a bachelor's or master's degree in architecture or another. Although graduate education beyond the professional degree is not essential for practicing architects, it is normally required for research, teaching, and certain specialties.

Architects must be able to visually communicate their ideas to clients. Artistic and drawing ability is very helpful in doing this, but not essential. More important is a visual orientation and the ability to conceptualize and understand spatial relationships.

Good communication skills (both written and oral), the ability to work independently or as part of a team, and creativity are important qualities for anyone interested in becoming an architect. Computer literacy is also required as most firms use computers for word processing, specifications writing, two- and three-dimensional drafting, and financial management. A knowledge of computer-aided design and drafting (CADD) is helpful and will become more important as architecture firms continue to adopt this technology.

During a training period leading up to licensure as architects, entry-level workers are called intern–architects. This training period gives them practical work experience while they prepare for the Architect Registration Examination. Typical duties may include preparing construction drawings on CADD, assisting in the design of one part of a project, or managing the production of a small project.

New graduates usually begin in architecture firms, where they assist in preparing architectural documents or drawings. They also may do research on building codes and materials or write specifications for building materials, installation criteria, the quality of finishes, and other related details. Graduates with degrees in architecture may also enter related fields such as graphic, interior, or industrial design; urban planning; real estate development; civil engineering; or construction management.

Salaries

Someone fresh from graduate school can expect to earn from $25,000 to $27,000 per year, depending of course upon the size of the firm, the importance of the project, and the region of the country. Advancement would depend upon ability and accomplishments. An experienced architect with five years or more at the project manager level could expect to earn about $40,000 a year in a mid-size firm. Those with specializations in demand can earn more. Most firms offer paid internships for graduate students.

Restoration Architects

A restoration architect, or an architect specializing in historic preservation, has experience similar to a general architect's. He or she understands how to plan spaces, how to organize construction materials, and how to put together construction documents. The difference between a general architect and a restoration architect is that the latter's work experience has primarily been focused on historic buildings. In addition, the restoration architect will have a specialized knowledge and understanding of federal, state, and local regulations with regard to historic preservation. They will also be aware of the standards set by the particular style of architecture.

The Nine Steps in a Restoration Project

1. The restoration architect first meets with the client and determines what his or her goals for the property are.

2. The restoration architect does an existing conditions analysis of the site; looks at the historical development of the building over time; and takes photographs, field measurements, and written notes.

3. Next, the restoration architect does a schematic plan, making preliminary drawings and sketches, describing a design to the client for approval. This stage could take four weeks or so.

4. Once the client approves the project, the restoration architect produces an outline of the scope of work and figures an order of magnitude cost estimate.

5. The next phase is to work on design development documents. This involves the use of more detailed drawings and can take from six to eight weeks.

6. Over the next eight to twelve weeks, construction documents including drawings and specifications are produced.

7. During the bidding phase the contractor is selected.

8. Construction plans are reviewed before actually beginning work.

9. The restoration architect makes frequent visits to the site while the project is in progress.

   Construction time varies but could take eight months to a year and a half depending upon the scope of the project.

What It's Really Like

Meet Peter Benton, Restoration Architect

Peter Benton earned a bachelor's degree in architecture in 1972 from the University of Virginia in Charlottesville. He worked for several years for various firms in Philadelphia and Washington, D.C., then went on to complete his master's of architecture at the University of Pennsylvania in 1979.

He is now a senior associate with John Milner and Associates, Inc., a mid-size architectural firm in West Chester, Pennsylvania, specializing in historic preservation. He joined the staff there in 1984 and has worked on a variety of projects.

Peter Benton's Background

"Initially I had relatively little training in preservation, but I was exposed to the idea of ecological planning at UPenn. I saw the philosophical connection between an ecological approach to the landscape and to the buildings, and that led me to historic preservation. I went to work for four or five years for an ecological planning firm and it was there my interest developed further.

"I've been responsible for all sorts of properties—anything from small, privately owned residential-scale houses from the eighteenth-century to high-style nineteenth-century mansions. In addition, I've worked with historic commercial and industrial buildings from the nineteenth-century, restoring them or practicing what we call adaptive reuse. For example, we recently converted an old mill into an office building and a farmhouse into a meeting facility. Another category I've worked with includes monumental buildings, such as a city hall or a large federal building."

Landscape Architects

Everyone enjoys attractively designed residential areas, public parks, college campuses, shopping centers, golf courses, parkways, and industrial parks. Landscape architects design these areas so that they are not only functional but beautiful and compatible with the natural environment as well. They may plan the location of buildings, roads, and walkways and the arrangement of flowers, shrubs, and trees. They also may redesign streets to limit automobile traffic and to improve pedestrian access and safety. Natural resource conservation and historic preservation are other important objectives to which landscape architects may apply their knowledge of the environment as well as their design and artistic talents.

Landscape architects are hired by many types of organizations, from real estate development firms starting new projects to municipalities constructing airports or parks. They are often involved with the development of a site from its conception. Working with architects and engineers, they help determine the best arrangement of roads and buildings. Once these decisions are made, landscape architects create detailed plans indicating new topography, vegetation, walkways, and landscape amenities.

In planning a site, landscape architects first consider the nature and purpose of the project and the funds available. They analyze the natural elements of the site, such as the climate, soil, slope of the land, drainage, and vegetation. They observe where sunlight falls on the site at different times of the day and examine the site from various angles. They assess the effect of existing buildings, roads, walkways, and utilities on the project.

After studying and analyzing the site, they prepare a preliminary design. To account for the needs of the client as well as the conditions at the site, they may have to make many changes before a final design is approved. An increasing number of landscape architects are using computer-aided design (CAD) systems to assist them in preparing their designs. Many landscape architects are also using video simulation as a tool to help clients envision the landscape architects' ideas.

Throughout all phases of the design, landscape architects consult with other professionals involved in the project. Once the design is complete, they prepare a proposal for the client. They draw up detailed plans of the site, including written reports, sketches, models, photographs, land-use studies, and cost estimates, and submit them for approval by the client and by regulatory agencies. If the plans are approved, landscape architects prepare working drawings showing all existing and proposed features. They also outline in detail the methods of construction and draw up a list of necessary materials.

Although many landscape architects supervise the installation of their designs, some are also involved in the construction of the site. However, this usually is done by the developer or contractor.

Some landscape architects work on a wide variety of projects. Others specialize in a particular area, such as residential development, historic landscape restoration, waterfront improvement projects, parks and playgrounds, or shopping centers. Still others work in regional planning and resource management; feasibility, environmental impact, and cost studies; or site construction. Some landscape architects teach at the college or university level.

Although most landscape architects do at least some residential work, relatively few limit their practice to landscape design for individual homeowners because most residential landscape design projects are too small to provide suitable income compared with larger commercial or multiunit residential projects.

Some nurseries offer residential landscape design services, but these services often are performed by less-qualified landscape designers or others with training and experience in related areas.

Landscape architects who work for government agencies do similar work at national parks, government buildings, and other government-owned facilities. In addition, they may prepare environmental impact statements and studies on environmental issues such as public land-use planning.

Training and Qualifications

A bachelor's or master's degree is usually necessary for entry into the profession. Many bachelor's of landscape architecture (B.L.A.) programs take five years to complete; a master's degree can take two or three years. The two-year master's program is designed for bachelor's level landscape architects; the three-year program is for students with bachelor's degrees in fields other than landscape architecture.

Your college curriculum will include the following courses:

History of landscape architecture

Landscape design and construction

Landscape ecology

Structural design

Drafting

Urban and regional planning

Design and color theory

Soil science

Geology

Meteorology

Topography

Plant science and other introductory horticulture courses

Civil engineering, including grading and drainage and pipe design

Construction law and contracts

General management

Pursuing a master's degree will help refine your design abilities, focusing on more complex design problems. It will also add greatly to your employability and salary prospects.

Almost all states require landscape architects to be licensed. Licensing is based on passing the Landscape Architect Registration Examination (LARE) sponsored by the Council of Landscape Architecture Registration Boards. Admission to the exam usually requires a college degree and at least one to four years of work experience. Some states, such as Florida and Arizona, require an additional exam focusing on the laws or plant materials indigenous to that state. Landscape architects employed by the federal government are not required to be licensed.

Before licensing, a new hire will typically be called a landscape architect intern. The title is misleading because interns can, depending upon their employer's requirements, perform all the duties of a licensed landscape architect. However, the intern will work under the guidance of a licensed practitioner until he or she has passed the exam.

Salaries

Statistics are limited, but salaries for entry-level bachelor's degree landscape architects start at about $22,000 per year. Those with master's degrees are able to add another $10,000 to their annual salaries.

What It's Really Like

Meet Kent Brinkley, Landscape Architect

Kent Brinkley is a landscape architect and garden historian at Colonial Williamsburg. He has been with the Foundation for more than ten years.

Kent Brinkley's Background

Kent Brinkley began his career with a B.A. in history from Mary Baldwin College in Staunton, Virginia. "I'm a dying breed—you see it less and less—but I came to landscape architecture through the back door. Just as lawyers used to be able to read the law under a licensed practitioner and then sit for the bar exam, years ago you used to be able to apprentice in a landscape architecture office under a licensed practitioner. It was an equal time commitment. In other words, when you got a five-year B.L.A. degree, you generally had to work in an office three years before you could sit for the exam. Or in lieu of that you could do eight years in an office and then take the exam. I waited ten years before I took the exam.

"I started as a draftsman and worked my way up to vice president of the firm before coming to Williamsburg."

On the Job

"I wear a lot of different hats. I sit at a drawing board and I do designs for new work that's taking place. We also have lots of gardens that were designed during the 1930s and 1940s by my predecessors, Arthur Shurcliff and Alden Hopkins. They did a lot of research and picked plants that were known and used in the eighteenth century. But in a few cases, a plant they chose, even though it was appropriate to the period, might not have been happy in a specific location because of too much sunlight or too much shade. So we try to come up with something else that would have been used but will grow better and flourish in that specific location.

"Many of these gardens are getting on in years. They're forty or fifty years old and, unlike the architecture where you just replace fabric when a board rots or you're putting a coat of paint on, plant materials do grow. They're dynamic and when you have a garden that's mature, or overmature as many of ours happen to be, part of my charge is looking at the replacements that inevitably have to be factored in when plants or trees die out. This keeps it looking presentable to the public.

"I work closely with Bob Scott, who is responsible for the maintenance. I provide the design expertise and we talk about what is needed in a particular garden. Once a decision has been made, Bob directs his maintenance staff to implement the work.

"I also spend time giving slide lectures to groups and garden clubs. I give garden tours a couple of times a month to the public just to have contact with the visitors on the street.

"I'm also a garden historian. That is someone who has a background in history and has done research and is interested in the development of the historical landscape over time. I've made any number of trips to England in the last fourteen or fifteen years and have visited many country estates and gardens over there. I've looked at English landscape design, which served as the precedent for many of the designs in the eighteenth century here in the Virginia Colony. Much of my work involves looking at what was done historically in gardens. The kinds of plants that were grown, how they were laid out, the types of fencing they were using—it's all part of knowing how to recreate a period garden.

"It's a specialty someone comes to within a history curriculum. It's a young field in this country; it didn't start as a discipline until 1975. If this interests you, you would combine history courses with horticulture courses. Of course the job market is fairly small, but it's growing. Right now most jobs are at living history museums such as Williamsburg, or Sturbridge Village and Plimouth Plantation in Massachusetts.

"When I got my job at Williamsburg, I was ecstatic. This was the perfect marriage of my love of history and my work as a landscape architect. It's been wonderful to be able to take two major interests and combine them in a way that allows you to do both."

Advice for Future Landscape Architects

"People who are mechanically inclined or are curious how things fit together and work would probably find landscape architecture and drafting to their liking. There is a lot of drafting involved; you have to know how to cultivate that drawing talent. You can get a leg up on the competition that way.

"You also have to have good English skills. You need the ability to write and speak well because you're working with people every day. You might have to get up in front of a group and make a presentation to sell your designs. Some sales ability is a good thing to have; you have to market yourself, your firm, and the design and be able to persuade people that this is the way to go. You can never waste your time by taking additional English or drawing courses.

"And I always advise students that once they've graduated, they should work in several different offices and get different kinds of experiences for the first five or six years. It's not a good idea to lock yourself into any one place. Some people study landscape architecture but they don't know what facet they want to pursue. They need time to test the waters before they'll know what their niche will be.

"And it's my personal recommendation to anyone coming into the field to work for two or three years before taking the licensing exam. It's comprehensive in scope and tests you on a variety of things. You need to get some experience under your belt before you try to tackle it.

"To conclude, I can tell students I think there's a bright future in the twenty-first century. For years the architects have beat their chests and said we're the guys who are going to save the world, but they haven't. They've done some pretty wretched designs. And then the engineers said they could do it, and though they certainly design functional work, they seem to have no feeling for aesthetics. So, now, there's a growing awareness that landscape architects may be the people to include on the design team. We are the ones who have a broad enough range of expertise to worry about environmental concerns and other things to make the resulting projects user-friendly and earth-friendly."

CHAPTER FIVE

Surveyors and Mapmakers

*I*n this chapter you will learn about several categories of surveying and mapmaking occupations that fit the perfectionist personality to a tee.

Areas of Specialty

Land surveyors establish official land, air space, and water boundaries. They write descriptions of land for deeds, leases, and other legal documents; define air space for airports; and measure construction and mineral sites. They are assisted by survey technicians, who operate surveying instruments and collect information.

Land Surveyors

Land surveyors manage one or more survey parties that measure distances, directions, and angles between points and elevations of points, lines, and contours on the earth's surface. They plan the fieldwork, select known survey reference points, and determine the precise location of all important features of the survey area. They research legal records and look for evidence of previous boundaries. They record the results of the survey, verify the accuracy of data, and prepare plats, maps, and reports. Surveyors who establish official boundaries must be licensed by the state in which they work.

The information needed by the land surveyor is gathered by a survey party. A typical survey party is made up of a party chief and several survey technicians and helpers. The party chief, who may be either a land surveyor or a senior survey technician, leads the day-to-day work activities. The party chief is assisted by survey technicians, who adjust and operate surveying instruments such as the theodolite (used to measure horizontal and vertical angles) and electronic distance-measuring equipment.

Survey Technicians

Survey technicians or helpers position and hold the vertical rods or targets that the theodolite operator sights on to measure angles, distances, or elevations. They may also hold measuring tapes and chains if electronic distance-measuring equipment is not used. Survey technicians also compile notes, make sketches, and enter the data obtained from these instruments into computers. Some survey parties include laborers or helpers to clear brush from sight lines, drive stakes, carry equipment, and perform other less skilled duties.

New technology is changing the nature of the work of surveyors and survey technicians. For larger projects, surveyors are increasingly using the Global Positioning System (GPS), a satellite system that precisely locates points on the earth using radio signals transmitted by satellites. To use it, a surveyor places a satellite receiver about the size of a backpack on a desired point. The receiver collects information from several differently positioned satellites at once to locate its precise position. Two receivers are generally operated simultaneously, one at a known point and the other at the unknown point. The receiver can also be placed in a vehicle to trace out road systems, or for other uses. As the cost of the receivers falls, much more surveying work will be done by GPS.

Mapping Scientists

Mapping scientists and other surveyors collect geographic information and prepare maps and charts of large areas. Mapping scientists, like land surveyors, measure, map, and chart the earth's surface but generally cover much larger areas. Unlike land surveyors, however, mapping scientists work mainly in offices and may seldom, if ever, visit the sites they are mapping.

Mapping scientists include workers in several occupations:

- *Cartographers* prepare maps using information provided by geodetic surveys, aerial photographs, and satellite data.

- *Photogrammetrists* prepare maps and drawings by measuring and interpreting aerial photographs, using analytical processes and mathematical formulas. Photogrammetrists make detailed maps of areas that are inaccessible or difficult to survey by other methods.

- *Map editors* develop and verify map contents from aerial photographs and other reference sources.

Some surveyors perform specialized functions that are closer to mapping science than traditional surveying.

- *Geodetic surveyors* use high-accuracy techniques, including satellite observations, to measure large areas of the earth's surface.

- *Geophysical prospecting surveyors* mark sites for subsurface exploration, usually petroleum related.

- *Marine surveyors* survey harbors, rivers, and other bodies of water to determine shorelines, topography of the bottom, water depth, and other features.

The work of mapping scientists is also changing due to new technologies. The technologies include the GPS, Geographic Information Systems (GIS), which are computerized data banks of spatial data, new earth resources data satellites, and improved aerial photography.

From the older specialties of photogrammetrist, or cartographer, a new type of mapping scientist is emerging. The geographic information specialist combines the functions of mapping science and surveying into a broader field concerned with the collection and analysis of geographic spatial information.

Working Conditions

Surveyors usually work an eight-hour day, five days a week, and spend a lot of time outdoors. Sometimes they work longer hours during the summer, when weather and light conditions are most suitable for fieldwork.

Land surveyors and technicians do active and sometimes strenuous work. They often stand for long periods, walk long distances, and climb hills with heavy packs of instruments and equipment. They are also exposed to all types of weather. Occasionally, they may commute long distances, stay overnight, or even temporarily relocate near a survey site.

Surveyors also spend considerable time in offices, planning surveys, analyzing data, and preparing reports and maps. Most computations and map drafting are done at a computer. Mapping scientists spend almost all their time in offices.

Engineering, architectural, and surveying firms employ nearly three-fifths of all surveyors. Federal, state, and local government agencies employ an additional one-fourth.

Major federal government employers are the U.S. Geological Survey, the Bureau of Land Management, the Army Corps of Engineers, the Forest Service, the National Oceanic and Atmospheric Administration, and the Defense Mapping Agency.

Most surveyors in state and local government work for highway departments and urban planning and redevelopment agencies. Construction firms, mining and oil and gas extraction companies, and public utilities also employ surveyors.

Training and Qualifications

Surveyors

Most persons prepare to be a licensed surveyor by combining postsecondary school courses in surveying with extensive on-the-job training. About twenty-five universities offer four-year programs leading to a B.S. degree in surveying. Junior and community colleges, technical institutes, and vocational schools offer one-, two-, and three-year programs in both surveying and surveying technology.

High school students interested in surveying should take courses in algebra, geometry, trigonometry, drafting, mechanical drawing, and computer science.

All fifty states license land surveyors. For licensure, most state licensing boards require that individuals pass two written examinations, one prepared by the state and one given by the National Council of Examiners for Engineering and Surveying.

In addition, they must meet varying standards of formal education and work experience in the field. In the past, many surveyors started as members of survey crews and worked their way up to licensed surveyor with little formal training in surveying. However, due to advancing technology and an increase in licensing standards, more formal education is now required. Most states at the present time require some formal post-high school education courses and five to twelve years of surveying experience to gain licensure. However, requirements vary among the states. Generally, the quickest route is a combination of four years of college, two to four years of experience (a few states do not require any), and passing the licensing examinations. An increasing number of states require a bachelor's degree in surveying or in a closely related field such as civil engineering or forestry with courses in surveying.

High school graduates with no formal training in surveying usually start as helpers. Beginners with postsecondary school training in surveying can generally start as technicians. With on-the-job experience and formal training in surveying either in an institutional program or from a correspondence school, workers may advance to senior survey technician, then to party chief, and finally, in some cases, to licensed surveyor (depending on state licensing requirements).

The American Congress on Surveying and Mapping has a voluntary certification program for survey technicians. Technicians are certified at four levels that require progressive amounts of experience; technicians who qualify are certified at a higher level after passing a written examination. Although not required for state licensure, many employers require certification for promotion to more responsible positions.

Surveyors should have the ability to visualize objects, distances, sizes, and other abstract forms and to work precisely and accurately because mistakes can be very costly.

Surveying is a cooperative process, so good interpersonal skills and the ability to work as part of a team are important. Leadership qualities are important for party chief and other supervisory positions.

Members of a survey party must be in good physical condition to work outdoors and carry equipment over difficult terrain. They also need good eyesight, coordination, and hearing to communicate by hand or voice signals.

Cartographers and Photogrammetrists

Cartographers and photogrammetrists usually have a bachelor's degree in engineering or a physical science, although it is possible to enter these jobs through experience as a photogrammetric or cartographic technician. Most cartographic and photogrammetry technicians have had some specialized postsecondary school training.

With the development of Geographic Information Systems, cartographers, photogrammetrists, and other mapping scientists now need more education and experience in the use of computers than in the past.

The American Society for Photogrammetry and Remote Sensing has voluntary certification programs for photogrammetrists and mapping scientists. To qualify for these professional distinctions, individuals must meet work experience standards and pass an oral or written examination.

Job Outlook

Employment of surveyors is expected to grow more slowly than the average for all occupations through the year 2005. In addition to openings arising from increased demand for surveyors, many will result from the need to replace those who transfer to other occupations or leave the labor force.

Growth in construction through the year 2005 should create jobs for surveyors who lay out streets, shopping centers, housing developments, factories, office buildings, and recreation areas. Road and highway construction and improvement also should generate new surveying positions. However, employment may fluctuate from year to year along with construction activity.

Some growth in employment of mapping scientists and other surveyors may occur in private firms; little or no growth is expected in the federal government.

As a result of the trend toward more complex technology, upgraded licensing requirements, and the increased demand for geographic spatial data (as opposed to traditional surveying services), there will be greater opportunities for surveyors and mapping scientists who have at least a bachelor's degree. New technology such as GPS and GIS may increase productivity for larger projects and may enhance employment opportunities for surveyors and survey technicians who have the educational background to use it, but limit opportunities for those with less education.

Salaries

In 1994, the median annual earnings for surveyors and mapmakers was about $30,600. The middle 50 percent earned between $21,800 and $43,600 a year. The median annual salary for survey technicians was about $27,000 a year in 1994.

In 1993, the federal government hired high school graduates with little or no training or experience at salaries or about $13,400 annually for entry-level jobs on survey crews. Those with one year of related postsecondary training earned about $14,600 a year.

Those with an associate degree that included courses in surveying generally started as instrument assistants with an annual salary of about $16,400.

In 1993, persons starting as land surveyors or cartographers with the federal government earned about $18,300 or $22,700 a year, depending on their qualifications. The average annual salary for federal land surveyors in 1993 was about $41,000, for cartographers, about $44,000, and for geodesists, about $47,600.

The average annual salary for federal surveying technicians was about $24,000, for cartographic technicians, about $30,100, and for geodetic technicians, about $37,300.

CHAPTER SIX

Engineers

E ngineers apply the theories and principles of science and mathematics to the economical solution of practical technical problems. Often their work is the link between a scientific discovery and its application. Engineers perform exacting tasks as they design machinery, products, systems, and processes for efficient and economical performance. They design industrial machinery and equipment for manufacturing goods and defense and weapons systems for the armed forces. Many engineers design, plan, and supervise the construction of buildings, highways, and rapid transit systems, working with architects and surveyors. They also design and develop consumer products and systems for control and automation of manufacturing, business, and management processes.

Engineers consider many factors in developing a new product. For example, in developing an industrial robot, they determine precisely what function it needs to perform, design and test components, fit them together in an integrated plan, and evaluate the design's overall effectiveness, cost, reliability, and safety. This process applies to products as varied as computers, gas turbines, generators, helicopters, and toys.

In addition to design and development, many engineers work in testing, production, or maintenance. They supervise production in factories, determine the causes of breakdowns, and test manufactured products to maintain quality. They also estimate the time and cost to complete projects.

Engineers often use computers to simulate and test how a machine, structure, or system operates. Many engineers also use computer-aided design systems to produce and analyze designs.

They also spend a great deal of time writing reports and consulting with other engineers.

Complex projects require many engineers, each working with a small part of the job. Supervisory engineers are responsible for major components or entire projects.

Engineering Specializations

Most engineers specialize. More than twenty-five major specialties are recognized by professional societies. Within the major branches are numerous subdivisions. For example, structural and transportation engineering, as well as environmental engineering, a small but growing discipline involved with identifying, solving, and alleviating environmental problems, are subdivisions of civil engineering.

Engineers also may specialize in one industry, such as motor vehicles, or in one field of technology, such as propulsion or guidance systems. Here are just a few of the engineering specializations available:

- Aerospace

- Architectural

- Biomedical

- Chemical

- Civil

- Computer

- Electrical and electronics

- Industrial

- Marine

- Materials, metallurgical, and ceramic

- Mechanical

- Mining

- Nuclear

- Petroleum

Engineers in each branch have knowledge and training that can be applied to many fields. Electrical and electronics engineers, for example, work in the medical, computer, missile guidance, and power distribution fields. Because there are many separate problems to solve in a large engineering project, engineers in one field often work closely with specialists in scientific, other engineering, and business occupations.

Some engineers work in management or sales, where an engineering background enables them to discuss the technical aspects of a product and assist in planning its installation or use.

Working Conditions

Many engineers work in laboratories, industrial plants, or construction sites, where they inspect, supervise, or solve on-site problems. Others work in an office almost all of the time.

Engineers in branches such as civil engineering may work outdoors part of the time. A few engineers travel extensively to plants or construction sites.

Many engineers work a standard forty-hour week. At times, deadlines or design standards may bring extra pressure to a job. When this happens, engineers may work long hours and experience considerable stress.

Employment Figures

In 1994, engineers held 1,327,000 jobs. Just under one-half of all engineering jobs were located in manufacturing industries, mostly in electrical and electronic equipment, aircraft and parts, industrial machinery, scientific instruments, chemicals, motor vehicles, guided missiles and space vehicles, fabricated metal products, and primary metals industries.

In 1994, 684,000 jobs were in nonmanufacturing industries, primarily in engineering and architectural services, research and testing services, and business services, where firms designed construction projects or did other engineering work on a contract basis for organizations in other parts of the economy. Engineers also worked in the communications, utilities, and construction industries.

Federal, state, and local governments employed about 181,000 engineers. Over half of these were in the federal government, mainly in the Departments of Defense, Transportation, Agriculture, Interior, and Energy, and in the National Aeronautics and Space Administration. Most engineers in state and local government agencies worked in highway and public works departments. Some engineers are self-employed consultants.

Engineers are employed in every state, in small and large cities and in rural areas. Some branches of engineering are concentrated in particular industries and geographic areas.

Training and Qualifications

A bachelor's degree in engineering from an accredited engineering program is usually required for beginning engineering jobs. College graduates with a degree in a physical science or mathematics may occasionally qualify for some engineering jobs, particularly in specialties in high demand. Most engineering degrees are granted in branches such as electrical, mechanical, or civil engineering. However, those trained in one branch may work in another. This flexibility allows employers to meet staffing needs in new technologies and specialties in short supply. It also allows engineers to shift to fields with better employment prospects, or ones that match their interests more closely.

In addition to the standard engineering degree, many colleges offer degrees in engineering technology, which are offered as either two- or four-year programs. These programs prepare students for practical design and production work rather than for jobs that require more theoretical, scientific, and mathematical knowledge. Graduates of four-year technology programs may get jobs similar to those obtained by graduates with a bachelor's degree in engineering. In fact, some employers regard them as having skills between those of a technician and an engineer.

Graduate training is essential for engineering faculty positions but is not required for the majority of entry-level jobs. Many engineers obtain master's degrees to learn new technology, to broaden their education, and to enhance promotion opportunities.

Nearly 340 colleges and universities offer a bachelor's degree in engineering, and nearly 300 colleges offer a bachelor's degree in engineering technology, although not all are accredited programs. Although most institutions offer programs in the larger branches of engineering, only a few offer some of the smaller specialties.

Also, programs of the same title may vary in content. For example, some emphasize industrial practices, preparing students for a job in industry, while others are more theoretical and are better for students preparing for graduate work. Therefore, students should investigate curriculums and check accreditations carefully before selecting a college. Admissions requirements for undergraduate engineering schools include courses in advanced high school mathematics and the physical sciences.

Bachelor's degree programs in engineering are typically designed to last four years, but many students find that it takes between four and five years to complete their studies. In a typical four-year college curriculum, the first two years are spent studying basic sciences (mathematics, physics, and chemistry), introductory engineering, humanities, social sciences, and English. In the last two years, most courses are in engineering, usually with a concentration in one branch. For example, the last two years of an aerospace program might include courses such as fluid mechanics, heat transfer, applied aerodynamics, analytical mechanics, flight vehicle design, trajectory dynamics, and aerospace propulsion systems. Some programs offer a general engineering curriculum; students then specialize in graduate school or on the job.

A few engineering schools and two-year colleges have agreements whereby the two-year college provides the initial engineering education and the engineering school automatically admits students for their last two years. In addition, a few engineering schools have arrangements whereby a student spends three years in a liberal arts college studying preengineering subjects two years in the engineering school and receives a bachelor's degree from each. Some colleges and universities offer five-year master's degree programs.

Some five- or even six-year cooperative plans combine classroom study and practical work, permitting students to gain valuable experience and finance part of their education.

Registration

All fifty states and the District of Columbia require registration for engineers whose work may affect life, health, or property, or who offer their services to the public. In 1992, nearly 380,000 engineers were registered. Registration generally requires a degree from an engineering program accredited by the Accreditation Board for Engineering and Technology, four years of relevant work experience, and passing a state examination. Some states will not register people with degrees in engineering technology.

Necessary Skills

Engineers should be able to work as part of a team, should be creative, and should have an analytical mind and capacity for detail. In addition, engineers should be able to express themselves well both orally and in writing.

Advancement

Beginning engineering graduates usually do routine work under the supervision of experienced engineers and, in larger companies, may also receive formal classroom or seminar-type training. As they gain knowledge and experience, they are assigned more difficult tasks with greater independence to develop designs, solve problems, and make decisions.

Engineers may become technical specialists or may supervise a staff or team of engineers and technicians. Some eventually become engineering managers or enter other managerial, management support, or sales jobs.

Some engineers obtain graduate degrees in engineering or business administration to improve advancement opportunities; others obtain law degrees and become patent attorneys. Many high-level executives in government and industry began their careers as engineers.

What It's Really Like

Meet David Martin, Senior Advisory Manufacturing Engineer

David Martin's specialization is automation. He works at Seagate Technology in Bloomington, Minnesota. Seagate Technology is the world's largest manufacturer and developer of hard disk drives. It is a more than $8 billion company and more than twice the size of the nearest competition.

David Martin earned his associate of science in electrical engineering technology from DeVry Institute of Technology in Phoenix, Arizona, in 1975. His bachelor of science was in electrical engineering from State University of New York, Stoney Brook, in 1976. He earned his master of science in mechanical engineering from Rensselaer PolyTechnic Institute in Troy, New York, in 1993 and his master of computer science from the University of Colorado in Boulder in 1996.

He is currently making application and taking graduate school courses towards a Ph.D. in control science and dynamical systems at the University of Minnesota in Minneapolis.

David Martin's Background

"I always enjoyed building things; even as a child, I played with Lincoln Logs, the Kenner sets, and finally Erector sets. I built literally hundreds of models from store-bought kits and constructed my own from scratch.

"I had an insatiable curiosity about how things worked. If I found an old junk TV or radio, I would bring it home—much to the chagrin of my mother—and tear it apart to see how it worked. I moved up to chemistry sets and biology sets, performing experiments that my mother was sure would blow up the neighborhood. I had a vast collection of biological specimens and performed dissections as early as the sixth grade. I had a set of encyclopedias, the *Young People's Science Encyclopedias*, I believe, and I read them from cover to cover until they were in tatters.

"When I was in the seventh grade, I knew that I wanted to be an engineer, to explore how things worked and design my own machines, mechanical and biological, and see the results. I spent the remaining years of my junior and senior high school years preparing for my training as an engineer.

"Electrical engineering was my first choice back then, as bio-engineering was only in its infancy and relatively unknown. Electrical engineering was considered the most difficult of the engineering disciplines, more mathematical and rigorous.

"It also held the most promise; the microprocessor was on the horizon and the impact that it would have on the world was just a glimmer. I wanted to be a part of that impact, that future.

"I majored in control systems, the mathematical branch of electrical engineering that deals with how systems function and how they are controlled. It varies, but in the United States about half of the universities that offer engineering degrees put control systems in the electrical engineering department, and the other half place control systems in the mechanical engineering department. (To complicate matters, some universities place control systems under aerospace engineering. Go figure.) I can't think of any university in the United States that has an undergrad program in control systems engineering, although the degree is quite common in Germany and France.

"It so happened that my undergrad university placed control systems in the electrical engineering department and my graduate school placed it in the mechanical engineering department. To be honest, I didn't know enough about control systems to really concern myself with it as a matter for selecting my undergraduate school. Later, of course, it was a different matter.

"So that should explain why I first studied electrical, then mechanical, engineering. However, any engineer who has interests in becoming a machine designer or automation engineer should seriously consider this multidisciplinary approach. Machine design requires a broad knowledge base; one must understand mechanics in order to design efficient control systems, and one must understand control systems in order to design machines that can be effectively controlled. It is rather a catch-22 situation, and you will find that most good machine designers have dual degrees in these fields.

"My Ph.D. program is rather unique. The University of Minnesota (which places control systems at the undergraduate level in the mechanical engineering department under the leadership of Professor Ogata, one of the foremost control system experts) has a unique doctorate program that is multidisciplinary. This is the only Ph.D. program in control science and dynamical systems. This program is administered by the following departments: electrical engineering, mechanical engineering, biomedical engineering, and computer science. The program is very heavily mathematical, and course selection is expected to include selections from at least three of the above four departments, as well as the mathematics department. A foreign language is also required.

"To give further evidence for the multidisciplinary flavor of this program, one has two faculty advisors from preferably two different departments. My advisors come from the electrical engineering and computer science departments.

"So if one was to classify me in one of the traditional areas of study, I would say that it would be safe to use the electrical engineering category. Of all of the disciplines, control systems is the most broad and comprehensive. Control systems are everywhere and in everything: from the household thermostat to the beating of our hearts, the complex control system in a modern jet fighter to the sense of balance in a child learning to ride a bicycle without training wheels. Control systems are the heart of mechanical and biological systems throughout the universe. That's where I wanted to be. I have followed that star throughout my professional and academic career.

"When I was in my senior year of college, I had become the sole means of support for my mother and brother. I needed to get a full-time job, and it looked as if I might have to drop out of school in order to survive. There was a company called Dynamic Science not too far from where I lived, so, on a lark, one day after work I dropped by and asked about a job. I had never applied for a job before—not counting high school summer jobs—and had no idea what to do. It was my lucky day. They were hiring test technicians for the night shift. I could keep going to school and work at the same time. The job involved the testing of vehicles, cars and trucks—destructive testing, crash testing. I held that job for three years, eventually becoming the chief test conductor, the youngest in the industry.

"Sadly, the company is no longer in existence, but to this day, I still consider that job the best I ever had, and I still have friends from there.

"For my current job, I was looking for a career position; that is, one that would offer the benefits and promotional path necessary for my long-term goals. The industry had to be viable, with excellent growth potential. This describes the computer disc drive business to a tee. I applied (I knew how by now), was granted an interview, and was nearly hired on the spot.

"The offer was overall the best one that I'd had in my career, and coupled with the opportunities offered, the right one as well."

On the Job

"I am the senior engineer in a group of tooling engineers: we design the machines that build the world's finest hard disc drives—The Seagate Barracudas. Automation is a rather exalted field; one must have knowledge of electrical and mechanical engineering, as well as computer programming. There is no room for specialization in this field. Consequently, the challenges can come fast and furiously. There is never a dull moment, and you can hardly wait to get back to work the next morning.

"A typical day would consist of answering problems and queries from our manufacturing facilities in the Far East that came in overnight—remember the time difference! These usually deal with the machine that I designed and have responsibility for. Then the current design projects—I currently have two prototype machines under design/construction. Progress must be checked, designs checked and modified, and designers, drafters, technicians, and other engineers given their work instructions.

"At my level of responsibility, there is more paperwork than I would like, but I always get into the lab each day and turn the wrenches and wire the control system. The machines are my creations, and I give them the personal care and treatment as if they were actual living things. (I know how Dr. Frankenstein felt.)

"Our business is extremely competitive. There can be a great deal of pressure. Our typical new product delivery cycle—from initial concept to full production—used to be eighteen months. It's now down to ten! There is pressure to perform accurately and with the utmost skill. Hours can be long, but the rewards are great.

"I recently finished the design of a balancing machine for the new Barracuda 9 drive, a nine-gigabyte drive that spins at 7200 rpm. It is the biggest, fastest disc drive in the world. (The founder of the company, Al Shugart, invented the hard disc drive over twenty years ago when he was at IBM. Al coined the term *hard disc drive* and spells disk as *d-i-s-c* in order to differentiate it from floppy *d-i-s-k* drives. Although other manufacturers—and remember they are much smaller and far less successful than Seagate—may choose to spell it as *d-i-s-k*.) Right now, sixteen of my balancers are helping to produce some seventeen thousand Barracuda 9s each day. Seventeen thousand! And my machines are running at upwards of 97 percent efficiency. No person could work as well as that machine. It's an incredible sense of satisfaction.

"I usually work fifty hours a week. My schooling—an engineer must always stay current in a rapidly changing technology—takes up about another twenty hours per week. The work atmosphere at Seagate is exceptional. Seagate is definitely an engineer's company. The accountants do not make the decisions here.

"I like the hands-on the most about my work. I love actually building the machines: getting dirty, lying on the floor under the electrical enclosure, pulling wire and cable, using my own two hands to create. That is unquestionably my favorite time. I spend more time in the lab than anyone else in my department.

"I like the paperwork and the meetings the least. I try to fol-low the advice of St. Dilbert: 'Avoid stupid meetings with time-wasting morons.' My manager nearly has to drag me to a meeting. I've tried every dodge short of feigning an injury to avoid a meeting. (And between you and me, I'm pretty darn good at it.)"

Advice from David Martin

"Engineering is a tough profession. Engineers are not well under-stood by other professions, especially accountants and lawyers. The general public has little conception of what we actually do, yet the result of our skill and labor touches the lives of everyone.

"If you want to be an engineer, you must love figuring out how something works, why it works, and how it can be made to work better. Engineers just love to change things.

"If you don't have that innate curiousity, then engineering is not for you. But if you do, then don't let anything stand in your way: not the science courses, not the math, not the work, and not the long hours of study. There is no profession that can offer such rewards for the time and energy you put into it.

"But the time and energy you must apply is great—this is not an easy job. It is mentally challenging and difficult. And it never gets easier. Easy is for managers. Easy is for accountants. Easy is for politicians and lawyers. Those people see the impossible task and say that it can't be done. Engineers see the impossible task and ask 'When do you want it done?'

"Engineers sent mankind to the moon—several times—and brought him back again. No one else but the engineer could have done that. Welcome to our ranks."

Meet Lisa Eagleson-Roever, Design Standards Specialist

Lisa Eagleson-Roever is an engineer and design standards spe-cialist at Cummins Engine Company in Columbus, Indiana.

Cummins designs and produces diesel engines for a variety of applications, including over-the-road trucks, light- and heavy-duty industrial, power generation, and marine equipment.

Lisa Eagleson-Roever earned her B.S. in physics in 1989 from Indiana University in Bloomington, Indiana. She earned her M.S. in aerospace engineering at Texas A&M University, College Station, in Texas in 1991. She has also taken aircraft accident investigation courses at the Transportation Safety Institute and a variety of diesel engine courses through Cummins Engine Company.

Lisa Eagleson-Roever's Background

"In college, as a physics major, I discovered that I wasn't nearly as interested in what is now professional physics as I was a more 'macro' aspect of physics—dynamics, forces, motion, fluids, systems interactions. The nice thing about physics is that it is wonderful at teaching problem solving, and it is a solid base for majoring in any other technical area. I couldn't decide whether to get a master's in physical oceanography (with a specialty in ocean currents and weather-related effects) or aeronautics (with a specialty in weather effects on aircraft, particularly the effects of icing on wings and rotors). Someone told me that if I went into oceanography, I'd have to take a lot of biology—which is my absolute worst subject—so I went for aeronautics.

"My first job was a three-month contract job in England for Dowty Rotol (now Dowty Aerospace Propellers). My graduate studies department and Dowty had a tradition of exchanging employees and graduate students. They would send employees for training and the university would send students for short-term contract jobs (if they were available). My turn came. I was asked if I wanted to spend the summer in England instead of Texas, and I said yes. The experience itself was invaluable.

"I loved icing. Although the aerospace and aeronautics degrees are lumped together under aerospace, my degree is really in fluid dynamics, which falls under the aeronautics category.

However, I graduated in December 1991, in the midst of the aviation/aerospace industry depression. The rest of the country was in a recession, but the aero-industry was in a true depression. Government contracts were drying up fast, new ones weren't appearing, and the small aircraft industry was suffering strong blows from what many people regarded as a flood of outrageously stupid lawsuits. Engineers with fifteen years' experience were willing to take entry-level jobs—and at entry-level pay—in an attempt to survive the fall and remain in the industry they loved. Someone like me, with almost no experience by comparison, had very little chance of getting a job back then. You can't blame these companies for making good business decisions. (Quotas? Forget it—there were no quotas. It was resume against resume, pure and simple. It still is, by the way.)

"So I went back to tutoring (something I'd done as an undergrad and a grad student), waited tables for a while (I was a truly awful server—my apologies to all my former customers), and then got a contract job as an engineer-in-training, that first crucial job title for a fledgling engineer. I wasn't doing much 'traditional' engineering, but I learned tons about writing, how to communicate with engineers, how to organize courses, and the theoretical aspects of what's involved in investigating aircraft accidents—from little Cessnas taken out by a private pilot and flown into a power line to huge airliners downed by the accumulation of many tiny, seemingly insignificant mistakes. I loved it. But the position was with a government agency, and they can't always keep contracts going forever, so I moved on to writing, researching, and editing for a law firm that specialized in aircraft industry litigation. This was also contract work, and it was fascinating. But it also ended.

"During this whole time, I never gave up entirely on getting a job as an engineer. When I waited tables, I worked late afternoons and nights so that I could be home to work on cover letters for resumes and answer the phone for phone interviews; I scrimped food money so that I could save up to buy two suits that

I could wear for my future engineering job; I bought the work clothes that I needed for waiting tables from the Goodwill Stores; I didn't go out with friends partying or drinking because I didn't want to lose what little I made on something that wasn't directed at getting that elusive engineering job. When I worked for the lawyers, I didn't have to scrimp food money anymore, but I tried not to spend too much. I never knew when the work would dry up.

"Finally, a headhunter I'd been sending resumes to for over a year called me up and tried to explain a job that had to do with writing engineering standards. I never really understood what the job itself was about, but knew it had to do with diesel engines (something I'd never studied but was willing to learn about) and writing (my lifelong passion). I wanted an engineering job badly, so I went to the interview. It was minus twenty-seven degrees Fahrenheit that day, with a minus-fifty-four-degree windchill, but I was out to get that job, come . . . well, you get the idea. I came in my best interview suit and heels. By the time I got from my car to the front gate of the plant, I could no longer feel my ankles—the wind was that cold. After all that, I was determined to understand what this job was (as I was being interviewed for it), and, if I liked it, sell them on the idea that I could do the job.

"I guess it worked. I got the job.

"I've explained how I fell into the position. As to why, well, the aero market is very, very tight (still) and the longer you're away from it, the less likely it is you'll ever get into it, so there's not much chance of my ever getting hired as an aeronautical engineer. It's been four and a half years since I graduated, and fluid dynamics is an area that grows continually. If you haven't done it for a year, you're out of touch with the area. I don't have much hope of going back to my former dreams."

On the Job

"Let me define a 'design practice' before I go on. A design practice is a set of guidelines for an engine component for all the current engine families made by my company. Design practices aren't so much strict do-it-this-way instructions as a set of keys for a good design: what systems will interact with this one, what design options are recommended, which are no longer recommended, what outside influences must you take into consideration as you design this component. (For example, are you designing a marine engine? Yes? Then will your materials be compatible with salt water? Here are some materials that have proven to work well with salt water. Here are some features you should design into your product because of the salt water. Here are some you should design into your product because the engine will be enclosed in a boat.)

"Design is a fluid business. With every new product, better ways to design a component are learned, so the 'keys' can be updated often. Getting that on paper can be hard, so Cummins is ahead of some other companies by having my group do this work.

"Because these practices cover all the engine families, I work with people from all over the world. These folks are very busy, and they are contributing their knowledge in between doing all the other things they already have to do. This means that I need to understand as much as I can about the topic before I talk to them, otherwise I'm perceived as a waste of their time.

"I have a lot of trouble describing my job so I've gotten to the point where I just say it's like mechanical engineering, because most of the people I work with are mechanical engineers. Technically speaking, if you'll excuse the unintended pun, I am in a support function. However, unlike most support functions, the minimum requirement for this job is a B.S. in any form of engineering or the equivalent experience. Engineers may have time to teach you the specifics of what they're doing, but they don't have time to teach you basic engineering.

"It used to be it was the design engineers who wrote the design practices. And there's nothing that says they can't, but they don't have the time to write them at the same level we do. Most of the old design practices were written by designers or developers for only one engine, because the engineer only knew one engine and didn't have the free time to research the good design practices that would apply to all the other engines. Furthermore, they didn't usually have time to update them, so eventually a design practice would become obsolete.

"That's why my group exists. We are engineers dedicated solely to the creation of design practices and the updating of the ones we create, so that they aren't neglected. It's part writing, part research, part diplomacy, and part group management. Every design practice is like a minicourse in a component. I'm learning the engine business one component and subsystem at a time. It's very autonomous—we make our own schedules and we are responsible for getting the job done by whatever method we need to use.

"Not only do I do a lot of writing, I also coordinate groups to gather the technical details of these design guidelines and handle the 'little things' that designers and production engineers don't have time to do: track down people, coordinate schedules, research technical reports, set up meetings, try to translate colloquial 'engineer-ese' into a more standard English that engineers at the overseas plants won't mistake for anything other than what is meant. (Try translating, "They're selling like hot-cakes" word for word and see what you get in Spanish or German or Russian. It will probably come out sounding very distasteful.)

"Sometimes even standard engineering phrases at one American plant mean something else at another American plant, so even though there's no translation concern, these groups still will have to decide on a mutually acceptable wording that, in itself, won't be misleading when translated.

"I also have to watch the technical content to make sure we're not trespassing on another design practice—or, worse still, contradicting one. This job would be hard for an English major to do, although many of the engineers I work with assume that I don't have an engineering degree. Most can't understand why anyone with a technical degree wouldn't just become a designer, like they are.

"But my job does have its advantages over specializing in design: My work hours aren't tied to a production schedule; I'm not delayed or rushed by parts suppliers' schedules; I have the chance to study all different parts of the engine; and I can meet more people in six months than some meet in two years. And it's hard to get bored in this job. If there's a component I find boring (which hasn't happened yet!), there are others I'm working on already, and when that component is done, I'll have others to do.

"It's very much a 'people-person' job. Getting people to participate is only half the 'diplomat' part of the job: keeping them interested in it and keeping a diverse group of people who may not agree on what is best from splintering into factions is far more challenging. Balancing the personalities in the group is essential, and often the key to getting the information you need and getting it down right the first time is to learn fast who can work together and who can't, and then to decide how to get input from those folks who don't work well together so that neither is shut out from participating. Sometimes the fastest way to do a project is to not have a group, but to work one-on-one with several people and coordinate the information as it comes in so that each gets to see what the others said.

"Even though I love to write, I can't have any 'story babies' in my job. Everything I write down will be subject to other engineers' scrutiny. And some can be very critical of what I've written, even if what I wrote is exactly what they said! Often it's not until they see it in print that they realize that what they said isn't what they were really trying to say. (That isn't limited to engineers, though.)

"Patience is essential. You have to check most of your ego at the door when you walk into a meeting you've called, but retain enough leadership skills to keep the meeting focused on its objectives. It's not so much physically demanding as mentally draining.

"What I like most about my job is the constant learning. This job allows me to keep learning something new all the time. It doesn't stagnate because of this. It's a fluid job and things change a lot, even though we do have a standardized method for the job we do. I'm always meeting new people, and I love to meet people from other countries. If I can, I try to learn about other cultures while I'm learning the technical information.

"What I like least about my job is that some engineers will assume that because I'm not a designer, I don't have the ability to understand what they have to tell me. I don't know if it's the job itself, or because I'm female, or both, but there have been times when I've had to bite my tongue to maintain a professional demeanor because someone has talked down to me so rudely or acted so patronizing that it was obvious this person thought I was a dimwit. I can't wear my diplomas on my sleeve—it can be challenging enough just being a female engineer without giving the impression that I'm a defensive female engineer—so I have to educate those who need educating politely and quietly, being careful not to make it look like I'm trying to embarrass the person. Some of the male engineers I work with simply don't know many female engineers, so it wouldn't occur to them I would be one. They aren't trying to be rude, really. And for those that are, there are ways of dealing with that too, but that is a controversial topic that every female engineer must decide for herself how to tackle.

"When I was in engineering school, I'd never heard of a position like mine. And even if I had, I probably wouldn't have wanted it. I really yearned to design helicopters or anything that could go on a helicopter."

Advice from Lisa Eagleson-Roever

"Use every opportunity you can during your undergraduate days to meet engineers—join professional organizations, go on every tour you can, collect business cards and quiz engineers by E-mail about their jobs, take any and all internships and co-op opportunities that come to you. Learn to write good paragraphs. Engineers who can effectively communicate ideas in simple, clear language (forget the techno-speak—we all hate it), will make higher salaries and have better job opportunities than those who can't write or speak well.

"Learn about the multinational connections of your branch of engineering and learn one of the languages that could be helpful in writing or speaking with an engineer from one of those countries. If you have the chance to go overseas—even if it's not for an engineering job—take it. The experience alone will give you a leg up on the students around you who don't have any international experience.

"Learn how to speak in front of a group. It doesn't matter if the only chance you get is talking to high schoolers about not drinking and driving—that counts, and probably more than giving a lecture on acoustics or materials technology. Getting a job in engineering is still tough, and you'll need to know how to learn what a company is looking for, how to translate what you've done into what they can relate to their job opening, and how to explain it to an interviewer in a concise, clear, professional manner. The more comfortable you are in speaking in front of a group, the easier it will be for you to survive an interview without sweating all over your interview suit.

"Don't assume you will or won't get a job because of the 'quota system.' Many industries are already 'balanced' and therefore don't need to follow a quota system. If you didn't get a job, write a letter and ask what qualifications you were lacking that the company was looking for. It may simply be that they really needed someone with a different background for that particular position, not that you wouldn't be qualified for any position at that same level. Many times people are willing to write back, and the tips they can offer can help you in the future. If you do feel like you were discriminated against, be careful about the action you take—people in the industry talk to each other, and you don't want bad things unduly attached to your name. If you think you should write the EEOC or the NAACP, then do it, but keep the letter professional and without emotional content. Write the facts (and only the facts) and ask for advice, but don't whine. You want to maintain your future employment opportunities while still making the industry a better place to be."

Job Outlook

Employment opportunities in engineering have been good for a number of years. They are expected to continue to be good through the year 2005 because employment is expected to increase about as fast as the average for all occupations while the number of degrees granted in engineering is expected to remain near present levels through the year 2005.

Many of the jobs in engineering are related to national defense. Defense expenditures have declined, so employment growth and job outlook for engineers may not be as strong as in times when defense expenditures were increasing. However, graduating engineers will continue to be in demand for jobs in engineering and other areas, possibly even at the same time other engineers, especially defense industry engineers, are being laid off.

Employers will rely on engineers to further increase productivity as they increase investment in plant and equipment to expand output of goods and services. In addition, competitive pressures and advancing technology will force companies to improve and update product designs more frequently. Finally, more engineers will be needed to improve deteriorating roads, bridges, water and pollution control systems, and other public facilities.

Freshman engineering enrollments began declining in 1983, and the number of bachelor's degrees in engineering began declining in 1987. Although it is difficult to project engineering enrollments, this decline may continue through the late 1990s because the total college-age population is projected to decline. Furthermore, the proportion of students interested in engineering careers has declined as prospects for college graduates in other fields have improved and interest in other programs has increased.

Only a relatively small proportion of engineers leave the profession each year. Despite this, three-fourths of all job openings will arise from replacement needs. A greater proportion of replacement openings is created by engineers who transfer to management, sales, or other professional specialty occupations than by those who leave the labor force.

Most industries are less likely to lay off engineers than other workers. Many engineers work on long-term research and development projects or in other activities which may continue even during recessions. In industries such as electronics and aerospace, however, large government cutbacks in defense or research and development have resulted in layoffs for engineers.

New computer-aided design systems enable engineers to produce or modify designs much more rapidly than previously. This increased productivity might have resulted in fewer engineering jobs had engineers not used these systems to improve the design process. They now produce and analyze many more design variations before selecting a final one. Therefore, this technology is not expected to limit employment opportunities.

It is important for engineers to continue their education throughout their careers because much of their value to their employer depends on their knowledge of the latest technology. In 1990, about 110,000 persons, or 7.5 percent of all engineers, were enrolled in graduate engineering programs. The pace of technological change varies by engineering specialty and industry. Engineers in high-technology areas, such as advanced electronics or aerospace, may find that their knowledge rapidly becomes obsolete. Even those who continue their education are

vulnerable if the particular technology or product they have specialized in becomes obsolete. Engineers whom employers consider not to have kept up may find themselves passed over for
promotions and are particularly vulnerable to layoffs.

On the other hand, it is often these high-technology areas
that offer the greatest challenges, the most interesting work,
and the highest salaries. Therefore, the choice of engineering
specialty and employer involves an assessment not only of
the potential rewards but also of the risk of technological
obsolescence.

Salaries

Starting salaries for engineers with bachelor's degrees are signifi-
cantly higher than starting salaries of bachelor's degree graduates
in other fields. According to the National Association of Colleges and Employers, engineering graduates with bachelor's
degrees averaged about $34,100 a year in private industry in
1994; those with master's degrees and no experience, $40,200 a
year; and those with doctorates, $55,300.

Starting salaries for those with bachelor's degrees vary by
branch, as shown in the following chart:

Petroleum	$38,286
Chemical	$39,204
Mechanical	$35,051
Nuclear	$33,603
Electrical	$34,840
Materials	$33,429
Industrial	$33,267

Aerospace $30,860

Mining $32,638

Civil $29,809

The average annual salary for engineers in the federal government in nonsupervisory, supervisory, and managerial positions was $58,080 in 1995.

CHAPTER SEVEN

Art Conservators

Perfectionists can put their skills to good use in the highly trained and specialized field of art conservation. Conservators work in museums and also as self-employed conservators. Art museum conservators work mostly with paintings or ceramics, for example, and natural history museum conservators work with a variety of objects and materials.

Many people think that once something valuable is in a museum it's safe, but unfortunately decay can happen on the museum's walls or shelves just as fast as in a private home. Many different conditions contribute to that decaying process: light, variations in humidity and temperature, pollutants, pests, and accidental damage.

Conservators, previously called art restorers, concern themselves with preventing deterioration through a number of steps:

1. Examination of the object to determine its nature, properties, method of manufacture, and the causes of deterioration

2. Scientific analysis and research on the objects to identify methods and materials

3. Documentation of the condition of the object before, during, and after treatment, and of actual treatment methods

4. Preventive measures to minimize further damage by providing a controlled environment

5. Treatment to stabilize objects or slow their deterioration

6. Restoration, when necessary, to bring an object closer to its original appearance

Teamwork

Being a conservator is a real team effort. Very often the conservator and curator call each other in and look under the microscope and discuss what they should do with a piece that's damaged, whether to leave it alone or just stabilize it to prevent further loss, but not pretty it up.

Conservators also work with the exhibits department. The conservator tells them how they can build a mount to support an object. They provide much of the information that is displayed on labels and arrange for proper lighting levels to prevent colors from fading.

Conservators also work closely with exhibit designers and curators when they're planning a new show or transporting objects. How an object is supported or wrapped for safe transportation to another museum often falls into the conservator's realm.

And though interacting with visiting scholars is generally part of a collection manager's job, conservators often instruct students in the correct way to handle an object.

What It's Really Like

Meet Joan Gardner, Chief Conservator

An objects conservator for a natural history museum will probably see a wider range of items than your average art museum conservator. Joan Gardner, chief conservator at the Carnegie Museum of Natural History, works with a comfortable variety of anthropological objects including skins, hides, fur, Indian robes, wooden dolls, and feathered headdresses.

Many of these garments and items were not meant to last longer than a few years, but some of them have now lasted several hundred. A conservator's efforts shows long-lasting results.

"We don't do a lot of restoration work," Joan explains. "We try to keep the object's integrity intact as much as possible. Restoration is often conceived of as trying to bring something back to its condition when it was new. That's not what we're after at all. We want to slow down further deterioration, but we're not necessarily someone who wants to put it back. We wouldn't take a sword that's ancient and make it shiny and look as if it were fabricated the day before yesterday. That's not our purpose. We want something to look cared for; we do care for the objects, and if they need treatment we will do it.

"But we'll document it and try to use only materials that are compatible and we know have proven to be reversible or will not interfere and cause some sort of contamination to the object. We try not to use any replacement pieces. If we have to, we try to use something compatible with the piece. We don't just arbitrarily use a new feather, for example, because it probably wouldn't be the right feather.

"At this particular time I'm working with a Hopi headdress that a child would wear. It's made of wood and painted, with feathers and leather straps. Then we have these huge headdresses from the Plains groups such as the Crow, the Arapaho, and the Lakota (formerly known as Sioux). They're made with dyed horse hair and eagle feathers and go from the top of the warrior's head and trail to the ground.

"I'm also dealing with Kachina dolls, which come from the Southwest. Most were produced by Hopi tribes, as well as others. They represent different spirits, usually made of wood, have an earthly component and spiritual component. The Hopi used them to get their gods to bring rain or fortuitous events, and as a training tool for children in the Hopi household.

"They have all kinds of accoutrements like bows and arrows and feathered headdresses. They're almost always painted and sometimes have outfits on that are very complicated.

"I'm also working on a bentwood box from the Northwest Coast Indian group named Haida. I do research into the materials it was made from, how it was made, the colorants—the red, the black, the blue, the green—what they are. We can take samples and send them off for analysis or you might use your own microscope to try to determine what the origin of the dye or paint was.

"The bentwood box is badly abraded and broken in many places and someone had previously hammered in steel nails all over it. Well, that's not compatible with what it looked like in the beginning. So, I won't touch it until I document what it looks like now, where the breaks are, where the new and modern materials have been used on it. Just to say it's a bentwood box doesn't tell you that much. We talk about the colors, the design, the technique that was used to cut out the design, the technique that was used to make it a bentwood box.

"We document its condition. We state, 'There's a fracture that's five millimeters long at the right corner. . . .' We take photographs of it before we work on it, during the time we work on it, and then after we're finished. What we're really trying to do is document what an object is made of, what we used on it, and why we did it, so there's a record for history. We're record keepers as well as people who intervene.

"After documenting its original condition, I will most likely remove those modern materials and use adhesives that are reversible, so in seventy-five years you can apply a little ethanol and get that adhesive out and put a different one in if something better comes on the market.

"I don't just shine it up and, if the red looks a little faded in a spot, I don't just put on some modern red. I will clean off soot and particulates, if I can without doing damage to the paint. But I'm not here to take a modern red and brighten it up.

"That doesn't mean that I wouldn't try to obscure some of the terrible abrasion points that when you look at it you think, 'Oh, isn't that in pitiful shape.' You would tone those down, but you would completely document what you've done so nobody misunderstands where you've been and what the original object was. You don't want to obscure the original artist's work at all.

"Here we have a real problem with particulates and soot. Pittsburgh has been an industrial city for a hundred years. That comes right through and settles on the objects unless they're enclosed. In the early days most objects were displayed on open shelves. They didn't have the great storage cabinetry we have now. One of our biggest jobs is try to remove the soot. It turns the objects practically gray and you can't see the vibrant blues and reds. To remove that without damaging the pigment or diluting it is quite a feat.

"For me, working with the objects is the best part of my job, dealing with the colors and the textures and the research to see what's happened to it in the past.

"It's such a constant challenge; as much as I love it, sometimes I get weary. It's a big job, overwhelming, and sometimes you can't really put it to bed at night. I do a lot of reading in the evenings to find out, for example, what the latest feather cleaning technique is. I go through a lot of journals to find an article that's pertinent. That for me is the only downside. I love what I do."

Joan Gardner's Background

Joan had been a science and math teacher and a social worker, then decided to change careers and went back to school as an adult. She was involved in a joint program with George Washington University and the Smithsonian Institution.

"My thesis director took me to the Smithsonian where they had just developed a program in museum studies with a conservation component. When I walked into the lab, I knew that that was what I wanted to do. I'd always been fascinated with anthropology and archeology in particular. You can't get into this profession without being fascinated with the objects that people produce in various cultures around the world, and what these objects mean, and why they're done the way they are. They're often so beautiful, but you just don't know, until you get into anthropology, what it all means. Sometimes you don't even know then.

"I was enrolled in a special studies program for my master's (the program is no longer in existence now) with an emphasis in conservation. It was split between anthropology and art history and I had a strong science background. There's an emphasis on a lot of chemistry.

"All programs have an internship. I did mine at the Smithsonian during the entire three years. It was almost a full-time job for me, fitting classes in between my hours at the Smithsonian. I got my master's in 1976 then came directly to Carnegie."

Training

Conservators are a group of highly trained professionals who have gone through a number of steps to gain their expertise. Training programs are few and, as a result, very competitive. According to the American Institute for Conservation of Historic and Artistic Works, the qualities a conservator must have are:

- appreciation and respect for cultural property of all kinds— their historic and sociological significance, their aesthetic qualities, and the technology of their production

- aptitude for scientific and technical subjects

- patience for meticulous and tedious work

- good manual dexterity and color vision

- intelligence and sensitivity for making sound judgments

- ability to communicate effectively

During the course of a training program, student conservators are exposed to working with a variety of materials before going on to specialize in a particular area. They learn skills to prevent the deterioration of paintings, paper and books, fiber, textiles, ceramics, wood, furniture, and other objects. There are even conservators in architectural conservation (see Chapter Five) and library and archives conservation.

Training is traditionally gained through a graduate academic program, which takes from two to four years. Apprenticeships or internships are a vital part of training and are usually taken during the final year of study. Some programs might offer internships that run concurrently with classes.

Admission requirements for the various graduate programs differ, but all of the programs require academic prerequisites, including courses in chemistry, art history, studio art, anthropology, and archeology.

Some programs prefer candidates to already have a strong background in conservation, which can be gained through undergraduate apprenticeships and field work in private, regional, or institutional conservation laboratories.

A personal interview is usually a requirement of the application process. A candidate's portfolio must demonstrate manual dexterity as well as familiarity with materials and techniques.

Careful planning at the undergraduate level will help improve the chances of acceptance into a graduate program, but because acceptance is very competitive, it is not unusual to have to repeat the application process. Before reapplying, however, it is a good idea to enhance your standing by undertaking additional studies or field work. Many programs, on request, will review your resume and suggest avenues for further study.

"It's expensive to train people in conservation and only a few are graduated each year," Joan Gardner says. "Before you go for your master's, you have to demonstrate a good knowledge of chemistry, you have to be good with your hands, and you have to be really bright. Almost every student has some talent, in painting, pottery, working with metals. Most people have a portfolio before they go on for their master's.

"Your master's will cover theory as well as practical experience. After your master's you can specialize. Usually by the time you're a third-year student you know what you want to specialize in. If, for example, you know you want to go into textiles, you find a museum and intern in the area of your interest. For instance, the assistant conservator here went through the Buffalo program and he spent two years working on all kinds of objects, doing theory, dealing with the different kinds of materials, and analysis, and special research projects. But he found that he really wanted to work with Native American material. So he did an internship at Arizona State Museum, a museum that specializes in anthropological objects, mostly ethnographic and archeology, so he was in just the right spot. Now he's here working with us as we get ready for our new Native American Hall.

"It's a wonderful profession but you have to have an awful lot of skill. I don't want to minimize that. Not only must you master the information, but you have to be able to deal with things that require an awful lot of patience. My master's work was unfolding and stabilizing some fabrics that were in a mound, buried in 1200 A.D. They were so dry, you would touch them and they'd shatter in your hands. Frankly, it's not something that most people have the patience for."

Conservation Degree and Internship Training Programs

The names and addresses of the fourteen conservation degree and internship training programs currently active in North America are listed in Appendix B. Contact those that interest you for their specific admission requirements.

Job Outlook

By the time you graduate with your master's, you will be a skilled conservator. Unfortunately, walking into a job in a natural history museum is not a shoe-in. "Not every natural history museum has a conservator," Joan Gardner explains. "Very often a museum will send their work to a private conservator because they can't afford to have a full-time conservator on staff. We do occasionally hire a private conservator to work with us. Now we have two private conservators working with us on the new Hall we're setting up. I couldn't possibly get all these objects ready by myself. I only have one assistant and I need help for this project.

"Some museums have two or three conservators for fine arts and/or objects. But a lot of the smaller ones don't have anybody.

"There are jobs out there but not nearly as many that there once were. A lot of new graduates go into private practice. Although it would be expensive for a new graduate to set up a private practice (the lab chemicals alone are very costly), once in practice, an independent conservator can do quite well."

CHAPTER EIGHT

Researchers

A researcher needs perseverance and an eye for detail and perfection. Just one more source, just one more resource until perfectionistic researchers are satisfied with the information they've managed to dig up.

Research is a large component of many of the jobs covered in this book. Actuaries, IRS agents, art conservators, surveyors, and writers, to name just a few, involve themselves in some way with research activity. In this chapter you will learn about genealogy as a career and also be introduced to several researchers whose jobs don't fall into any of the expected categories.

Genealogists

The study of genealogy, tracing family histories, has recently become one of the most popular hobbies in the United States. Many people share a keen interest in their family backgrounds. Many genealogy hobbyists take their interest one step further and become self-employed genealogists, helping others to dig up their family trees. Genealogists also are employed in historical societies and libraries with special genealogy rooms.

The Church of Jesus Christ of Latter Day Saints in Salt Lake City, for example, has a huge repository of family information in a subterranean library. The organization employs genealogists all over the world and includes genealogists who have been accredited through its own program on a list of freelance researchers. For more information write:

Accreditation Program
Family History Library
35 N West Temple Street
Salt Lake City, UT 84150

Other genealogists find work teaching their skills to others in adult education classes or by editing genealogy magazines or writing books or newspaper genealogy columns.

Most genealogists are not formally trained, though specializing in genealogy is possible through some university history and library science programs. In addition, a genealogist can become board certified. For information on certification requirements and procedures, write to:

Board for Certification of Genealogists
P.O. Box 5816
Falmouth, VA 22403-5816

Salaries

Salaries vary depending upon the institution where a genealogist is employed and upon the individual's level of expertise. Self-employed genealogists make anywhere from $15 to $35 an hour.

Getting Started

The National Genealogy Society makes the following suggestions for beginners:

1. *Question older family members.* Encourage them to talk about their childhoods and relatives and listen carefully for clues they might inadvertently drop. Learn good interviewing techniques so you ask questions that elicit the

most productive answers. Use a tape recorder and try to verify each fact through a separate source.

2. *Visit your local library.* Become familiar with historical and genealogical publications (a few sources are provided at the end of this chapter and in the appendix) and contact local historical societies and the state library and archives in your state capital. Seek out any specialty ethnic or religious libraries and visit cemeteries.

3. *Visit courthouses.* Cultivate friendships with busy court clerks. Ask to see source records such as wills, deeds, marriage books, birth and death certificates.

4. *Enter into correspondence.* Write to other individuals or societies involved with the same families or regions. Contact foreign embassies in Washington, D.C. Restrict yourself to asking only one question in each letter you send. Include the information you have already uncovered. Include a self-addressed stamped envelope to encourage replies.

5. *Become computer literate.* Members of the National Genealogical Society can participate in a special computer interest section. It encourages the use of computers in research, record management, and data sharing.

6. *Keep painstaking records.* Use printed family group sheets or pedigree charts. Develop a well-organized filing system so you'll be able to easily find your information. Keep separate records for each family you research.

7. *Write the National Genealogical Society.* Take advantage of the society's forty-six-page book (*Beginners in Genealogy*), charts, and library loan program. You can also enroll in their home study course called, *American Genealogy: A Basic Course.*

What It's Really Like

Meet Valarie Neiman, Academic Researcher

Valarie Neiman formed EVN Flow Services in 1993. Through her home-based business she does academic, business, and creative writing and provides research and editing services.

She earned her B.S. in business administration (transportation) in 1980 from Arizona State University in Tempe and her M.A. in human resources development in 1993 from Ottawa University in Phoenix.

Valerie Neiman's Background

"Research isn't what I do, it's part of who I am. As one of the original latch-key kids in the 1950s, I spent a lot of time reading when I got home from school. To avoid being bored in class, I'd always read ahead in the textbooks. My first job fresh out of high school in 1966 was typing resumes. Surprising how little they've changed in thirty years. The woman I worked for began letting me write them, and soon, I did the interviews as well.

"After a variety of clerical and secretarial jobs, I went back to school in my mid-twenties and earned a bachelor's degree in business. Eventually, while working for a major defense contractor, I began work on a master's. I was excused from the employer, who had been paying my tuition, and went on to temporary positions—from management consultant back to typist. Bummer!

"My final temp assignment was researching and writing warehouse procedures. I convinced the manager that it would be cheaper to hire me as an independent contractor rather than pay the temp agency. At the same time, I put up a notice at my alma mater offering to help students with their research projects.

"The rest, as they say, is history. When I began EVN Flow (Ellwood and Valarie Neiman keep work flowing), my current business, I expected to help students format and type their papers. However, adult learners (over twenty-five) often haven't had training or don't remember how to write research papers. My work soon evolved into 'filling in the gaps' in their abilities. Part of the job is reassuring them that they aren't stupid, letting them know I've developed a unique (and marketable) talent for pulling their work together into a package that makes them look good.

"The work I do is enjoyable because every day is different and every project takes me on a new path. Had I realized years ago that I am what is gently referred to as an 'individual contributor' I may have found my niche sooner. I prefer to work alone, without supervision. I focus on the task at hand and am goal-oriented enough to get it done so I can move to the next project.

"People may think of researchers as scientists or academics. I believe research is an element in almost every job, whether dealing with things, people, or ideas. Most of the time, though, it isn't thought of as research.

"To me, the distinction of a job as a researcher is that the goal is to present knowledge in a different way, consolidate facts and assemble them to make a point, discover new relationships in existing knowledge, or develop background and authenticity—in creative writing, for example.

"One of the things I like least about my work is that it isn't full-time and can be seasonal. I began writing a novel to fill those dreaded unbillable hours. Of course, the part-time nature of the work is also one of the things I like best! I'm sure that others in various types of research positions make a living. By my own choice, I make enough to pay business expenses and to pay myself a small stipend. Because I am a business, travel, postage, supplies, and capital equipment associated with my writing are all considered expenses.

"My business is home based. I have one employee (my husband), who is financial manager and gofer. We share a large office and one mother-ship computer and I have an old laptop for plain old writing.

"I tutor adult learners in planning, researching, and writing academic papers. I review and edit master's research and graduation review projects. I am under contract with Ottawa University to read and edit first drafts of master's candidates' theses.

"I also collaborate on research and writing a series of booklets on pricing, niche marketing, networking, outsourcing, tax tips, and how to start a home-based business (published by the Home-Based Business Association of Arizona, HBBA).

"My time is mine to spend as I wish. Since I like variety and 'big' projects, I find I work for an hour or so on one, then shift to another, and so forth. Some days, I catch up on phone calls or maintenance, but if I have paying clients, I stay focused on them. Some days I work fourteen hours (rare), others only three or four. I have a wonderful, understanding boss."

Advice from Valerie Neiman

"Read, read, read, research, research, research. Go to the library, get on-line, practice finding things. Interview people, create questionnaires, read magazines.

"The key requirement for a life of research is a desire, not to say compulsion, to *know*. In addition, a researcher (whether scientific, academic, or journalistic) needs persistence, judgment, empathy, and intuition. A researcher must establish limits and develop shortcuts or the process goes on forever, each step leading to another source, ad infinitum.

"A researcher with broad experience is more likely to be exposed to a variety of sources—not just the public library. I've worked in government, major corporations, and small businesses. Each job provided a whole new set of resources that I am now able to draw upon.

"How to get a research job? The possibilities are endless, but chances are good there won't be an ad in the newspaper. *Researcher* is more an activity than a job title. It's the same old story. Network, create an excellent resume, and research your prospects.

"A college degree or three is probably a good start (up to and including a Ph.D. or post doctoral). The major doesn't matter. A student who thrives in an academic environment will likely have the curiosity and temperament to excel as a researcher.

"With the emphasis on education (to keep youngsters out of the job market as long as possible), even a fact checker at a newspaper or magazine would probably need a degree.

"Hone those writing skills. Research is useless without presenting results. Facts are just data. A researcher worth his or her salt must be able to interpret the facts and consolidate or extrapolate them into usable information.

"And remember, in scientific or social research especially, the honesty and ethics of a researcher must be unquestioned. A researcher must maintain the confidentiality of people and ideas."

Meet Susan Broadwater-Chen, Information Specialist/Freelance Writer

Susan Broadwater-Chen owns Moonstone Research and Publications, her own home-based business in Charlottesville, Virginia. She has a B.A. in humanities from Asbury College in Wilmore, Kentucky, and her master's in theological studies from Emory University in Atlanta, Georgia.

Susan Broadwater-Chen's Background

"I have an insatiable curiosity about just about everything and I love to write. I especially like the challenge of having to find something and the excitement that comes when I find it. I love libraries, books, and puzzles and some of the searches that I do are very much like putting puzzles together.

"I attended Mountain Empire Community college in Southwest Virginia in the early 1980s and took as many computer courses, including programming, as were offered. After finishing those courses, I took a job at the University of Virginia as a program support technician and part of my job was doing a lot of editing and spending a lot of time working with research assistants.

"Eventually I took courses through UVA on how to navigate the Internet and do Web pages. I worked at UVA for ten years and ran a business out of my home doing everything from research to editing during that time.

"I started in 1986 on a part-time, moonlighting basis. I've been full-time since 1995. I had built up enough contacts and customers that I could become independent and I quit my job at UVA and started publishing a monthly newsletter and running a Web page. When I realized that I could support myself by using my skills to expand my client base, I decided to devote myself full-time to this business.

"Currently, I publish a monthly newsletter that focuses on Internet materials that writers will find useful. I also take individual research projects from authors who are looking for information that is proving hard for them to find on their own.

"In addition, I work with a couple of on-line author colonies/workgroups in developing content for research libraries. This includes going through antiquarian books, microfilm, and other sources to provide both primary source materials and bibliographical information. My company has a storefront on the Internet where writers or anyone else can download some materials for free and pay for others. I offer a clipping service for subscribers and hold a weekly workshop on-line to help people with any questions they might have about finding what they are looking for.

"The job is very demanding. Most of my customers can't wait a week or two for what they are looking for. In addition, putting out a large newsletter each month and submitting articles to at least one on-line magazine each month is very time consuming. I begin my day at 6:00 A.M. and, as my son eats his breakfast, I check my E-mail, writing down every request that comes through on a special pad. After that I check the newsgroups/news services to see if there is anything I need to come back to later and deleting what I don't want to look at.

"After I get my son on the bus, I come back and print the articles I want to read or save. As soon as that is done I file them in topical folders. You have to be organized in this job or you are doomed to have all kinds of paper and not know how to put your hands on what you really need when you need it. I keep a folder of things I may want to review or talk about in my newsletter and the rest is filed by topic.

"Next, I work on the products I intend to sell. This means reading and writing articles or finding out-of-copyright primary source material that can be edited and reprinted for sale. I try to do a minimum number of these products a day. After that is finished, I turn to the content I am developing for the on-line services. When that is finished, it's time to check E-mail again and to start working on the requests I have received overnight. I walk after that because I need time to myself and away from my desk.

"When I come back to work, I write at least one review or article for my newsletter and then start exploring potential Internet sources that I may want to review. I take notes and make printouts and put this aside to be written up the next day. Next, I telnet into library card catalogs looking for materials that I may want to request on inter-library loan from my local library and write down information on those books. Because I work at home it's a relaxed atmosphere, but sometimes I feel really pressured because there seems to be so much to do and only a limited number of hours in a day. I usually work about eighty hours a week, which is forty more than when I worked for someone else. I have one morning that I spend in the library every week. The job is not boring but it's not easy money either.

"I like it when I can help somebody and it makes me feel good to know that they are happy with what I've found for them. When I've helped a person who is publishing books and they send me a copy of their book, I get personal satisfaction knowing that I've helped them with the research that their book required.

I also like the feeling I get when I find some really obscure fact and pull the needle out of the haystack. The downside is that sometimes I can't help someone because the facts won't bear out what they want to write about."

Advice from Susan Broadwater-Chen

"It's not an easy job. You need to learn all you can about electronic databases and the Internet. In addition, you need to learn all you can about how to find information in your library and from interviewing people.

"You can't have a business based on doing Internet research alone. You have to cultivate as many skills as possible and know where to look for specific material. It's also important to build up a client base and connections before you take this on full-time. Volunteer to do things for groups who might need your services on the Internet and on-line services. Submit articles to on-line publications and start networking with people in professions or with interests who might need your services."

CHAPTER NINE

Writers and Editors

T he United States supports the largest mass media system of any country in the world, which in turn has generated millions of jobs. The choices for perfectionists wanting to work in this wide-open field could almost be daunting if it weren't so exciting.

The field of journalism is perhaps the most obvious path open to those who have writing and editing talent, but no longer does the "fourth estate" refer only to newspapers. It includes syndicates and wire services, television and radio, consumer and trade publications. And while these outlets provide a home for journalists to report and interpret the news, they also furnish niches for creative writers with a vast array of specialties, as well as editors, agents, entertainers, broadcasters, producers, photographers, computer experts, and other important frontline and support positions.

The Paths You Can Take

Because there is such a vast range of jobs within the media, and many of those same positions are found in several different outlets, it is more efficient here to examine each outlet as a career path onto itself. While the role of editor, for example, will vary to some degree depending upon the setting, many of the same functions are performed and the same skills utilized in newspapers as well as magazines. The definitive question is not whether to become an editor, but in which milieu will the future editor be most satisfied working.

Similarly, a hopeful writer will benefit from knowing the types of assignments and working conditions involved at the different job settings or whether a career as a freelancer is a viable alternative. For every interest there is a job and a setting to satisfy it.

Job titles within the print media cover the gamut of writers, editors, entertainers, production people, and a host of other professionals. This list is not mean to be exhaustive. You can add to the list yourself or find additional related job titles and descriptions in *The Dictionary of Occupational Titles* (U.S. Department of Labor).

Acquisitions Editor	Desk Assistant
Art Director	Dramatic Agent
Assignment Editor	Editor
Assistant Editor	Editorial Assistant
Associate Editor	Editorial Writer
Author	Editor in Chief
Book Editor	Electronic Publishing Specialist
Bureau Chief	Executive Editor
Bureau Reporter	External Publications Editor
City Editor	Feature Writer
Columnist	Freelance Editor
Contracts Assistant	Freelance Writer
Copyeditor	Internal Publications Editor
Copywriter	Investigative Reporter
Correspondent	Journalist
Critic	Literary Agent

Managing Editor	Section Editor
News Editor	Senior Editor
Newspaper Editor	Senior Writer
News Writer	Staff Writer
Photojournalist	Story Editor
President	Stringer
Production Editor	Syndicated Columnist
Publisher	Technical Editor
Reporter	Wire Editor
Researcher	Writer

Newspapers

Current figures show that there are approximately 9,200 news-papers in the United States; 1,700 are dailies, most of which are evening newspapers, the remainder are weeklies. The number of major dailies has declined in recent years; there are only about thirty-five newspapers with a circulation of more than 250,000. Despite declining numbers, newspapers rank as the third largest industry in the United States and employ 450,000 people.

Newspapers are usually organized around the following departments: news, editorial, advertising, production, and circulation. All provide job opportunities for writers and editors.

The News Department

A job as a reporter is viewed as a glamorous and exciting Clark Kent/Lois Lane type of existence and probably attracts more applicants than any other spot on a newspaper staff. As a result competition is stiff; reporters make up less than one-fourth of a newspaper's roster.

Reporting is challenging and fast paced with the pressures of deadlines and space allotments always looming overhead. For those who like to be one step ahead of the general public in knowing what's going on, it's the ideal job.

Whatever the size or location of the newspaper, the job of reporters is to cover local, state, national, and international events and put all this news together to keep the reading public informed. News reporters could be assigned to a variety of stories, from covering a major world event to monitoring the actions of public figures to writing about a current political campaign.

The Editorial Department

Newspaper editorial sections vary with size and location but most include at least some, if not all, of the following sections:

Art	Health
Business	International News
Books	Lifestyles/Features
Consumer Affairs	Local News
The Courts	National News
Crime Desk	Religion
Education	Science
Entertainment	Social Events
Fashion	Sports
Finance	State News
Food	Travel
Foreign Affairs	Weather

Staff Writers

Staff or feature writers function in much the same way as news reporters but are generally assigned a regular "beat" such as health and medicine, sports, travel, or consumer affairs. Working in these specialized fields, staff writers keep the public informed about important trends or breakthroughs in a variety of areas.

Contrary to some misconceived notions, feature writers are not assigned only to fluff pieces. While a fashion writer might not do in-depth investigative pieces, a health and medicine writer can. Nancy McVicar, for example, is a senior writer at the *Sun-Sentinel*, a newspaper in Fort Lauderdale, Florida, with a circulation of about one million. She works for the Lifestyle section, which has a health page every Thursday, and her work has been nominated for the Pulitzer Prize seven times. Several of her stories have won other prestigious national awards.

McVicar was the first to break the story "Are Your Cellular Telephones Safe?" She produced two or three articles on the topic, which went out over the wire and also ended up on *20/20* and *60 Minutes*. The GAO (General Accounting Office of the U.S. government and also the investigative arm of congress) was asked to do an in-depth report on whether or not cellular phones are safe, based on the stories she wrote.

Writers in every section of a newspaper can find a way to make an impact.

Section Editors

A job as a section editor is considered by many to be a plum position. Although there are exceptions, section editors have usually paid their dues as reporters or staff writers, and only after a few years of experience would be eligible for consideration.

The duties involved depend in part on the section, but there are many responsibilities in common. Editors write articles or supervise the work of staff writers, making assignments, reviewing copy, and making sure attention is paid to space requirements. They also attend editorial meetings and correspond with freelance writers.

There are many perks associated with some of the sections; travel writers get to travel, book editors get free books in the mail to read and review, sports editors go to a lot of the games, food editors get to eat, society page editors are invited to a myriad of social events, and so on.

Working Conditions

Reporters and photojournalists always have deadlines hanging over their heads. Unlike fiction writers, who can work at their own pace, reporters do not have the luxury of waiting for their creative juices to begin to flow. A news reporter has to file a story, or maybe even two, every day by a certain time. A staff writer or section editor with a weekly column has more leeway, but still, everything must be in on time to go to press.

Reporters gather information by visiting the scene, interviewing people, following leads and news tips, and examining documents. While some reporters might rely on their memory, most take notes or use a tape recorder while collecting facts. Back in the office, they organize their material, decide what the focus or emphasis should be, and then write their stories, generally using a computer. Because of deadlines, while away from the office, many reporters use portable computers to file the story, which is then sent by telephone modem directly to the newspaper's computer system.

Some newspapers have modern, state-of-the-art equipment; others do not have the financing they need to update. A reporter could work in a comfortable, private office, or in a room filled with the noise of computer printers or coworkers talking on the telephone.

Working hours vary. Some writers and editors could work Monday through Friday, nine to five, while others cover the evenings, nights, and weekends. On some occasions, reporters work longer than normal hours to cover an important ongoing story or to follow late-breaking developments.

Although there is some desk work involved, newspaper report-ing is definitely not a desk job. Reporters have to have excellent interviewing and research skills and the ability to juggle several assignments at once. Computer and typing skills are very impor-tant, too.

A reporter also must know how to "write tight." While feature writers can be more creative, news reporters must make sure they get all the facts in within a certain amount of space. The editor might allocate only a column inch or two for a story, leaving room for just the who, what, when, where, why, and how.

Training and Qualifications

A college degree is a must; most employers prefer a B.A. in jour-nalism or communications, while others would accept a degree in a related field such as political science or English.

The courses you take in college should include introductory mass media, basic reporting and copy editing, history of journal-ism, and press law and ethics.

Previous work on a school paper or an internship at a newspa-per will help to enhance your resume. Experience as a "stringer"—a part-time reporter who is paid only for stories printed—is also helpful.

Photojournalism is highly competitive so a good portfolio is very important. Most photojournalists have at least a bachelor's degree; many, especially those with management inclinations, have a master's.

Career Outlook

Jobs working for newspapers are expected to grow in the next ten years or so, especially with the small town and suburban dailies and weeklies. But competition for jobs on the large urban news-papers will continue to be fierce.

Editors prefer to hire top graduates from accredited programs. A beginning reporter would probably have better luck starting out at a small paper, gaining a year or so of experience, and then moving on. Reporters have to be prepared to move to where the jobs are. You could waste a lot of time waiting for that plum position to open up at your hometown paper. You don't want to have six different jobs in three years—you should stay at a paper long enough to utilize everything they have to offer.

Salaries

The Newspaper Guild negotiates reporters' wages with newspapers, both the starting minimum salary and the top minimum, which takes effect after three to six years of employment. Variations in salary will occur depending upon the region of the country in which you work. There are certain cities, such as New York and Washington, where wages are higher, but the cost of living is also much higher.

A beginning reporter at a small paper could start at about $15,000 a year. In a big city, a reporter could start with a salary of $25,000 or so. The average top minimum salary for a reporter with a few years experience is about $34,000 to $40,000 a year. Salaries for editors usually run higher, but those positions are generally not available to those just starting out.

Magazines

Visit any bookstore or newsstand and you will see hundreds of magazines covering a variety of topics—from sports and cars to fashion and parenting. There are also many you won't see there—the hundreds of trade journals and magazines written for businesses, industries, and professional workers in as many different careers.

These publications all offer information on diverse subjects to their equally diverse readership. They are filled with articles and profiles, interviews and editorials, letters and advice, as well as pages and pages of advertisements.

Whether you work for a magazine full-time or as an independent freelancer, you will discover that there is no shortage of markets where you can find work or sell your articles. Positions within magazines are very similar to those found in newspapers.

Freelance Writing

A freelance writer works independently, in rented office space or in a home office. Most freelance writers plan and write articles and columns on their own and actively seek out new markets in which to place them.

Staff writers for newspapers and magazines might have less freedom to choose what they write, but they generally have more job security and always know when their next paycheck will arrive. Freelancers trade job security and regular pay for their independence.

Both freelancers and those permanently employed have to produce high quality work. They have editors to report to and deadlines to meet.

More and more magazines are open to working with freelancers these days. With budget cuts and staff layoffs, and because magazines don't have syndicated material to fall back on, it is generally less expensive to pay several different freelance writers by the piece, rather than employ a full-time staff writer or two.

Some freelancers are generalists; they will write about anything they think they can sell. Others are specialists, choosing to write only in a particular field such as travel, or health and medicine. Successful freelancers have a lot of market savvy; that means they are familiar with all the different publications they could market their work to and know how to approach those publications.

Training and Qualifications

While many writers hone their writing craft in college, the business of freelancing is generally self-taught. There are, however, adult education classes throughout the country, as well as writers' associations, that can provide new freelancers with some guidance and marketing strategies.

Before starting, read as many magazines as you can, and in particular, those you would like to write for. It's never a good idea to send an article to a magazine you have never seen before. Being familiar with the different magazines will also help you to come up with future article ideas.

Once you have decided what you want to write about, there are two ways you can proceed. You can write the entire article "on spec," send it off to appropriate editors, and hope they like your topic. Or, you can write a query letter, a mini-proposal, to see if there is any interest in your idea first. Query letters will save you the time of writing articles you might have difficulty selling. Only once you're given a definite assignment do you then proceed.

You can find out about different magazines and the kind of material they prefer to publish in the market guides listed at the end of this chapter.

Earnings

Getting a check for an article can be rewarding, but sadly, for new freelancers, the checks might not come often enough and are not always large enough to live on.

While staff writers are paid a regular salary (though generally not a very high one), a freelancer gets paid only when an article sells. Fees could range from as low as $5 to $1000 or more depending upon the publication. But even with a high-paying magazine, writers often have to wait until their story is published before they are paid. Because publishers work so far ahead, planning issues six month or more in advance, payment could be delayed from three months to a year or more.

To the freelancer's advantage, sometimes the same article can be sold to more than one magazine or newspaper. These resales help to increase income. You can also be paid additional money if you can provide your own photographs to illustrate your articles. Freelance writers don't need a long, impressive resume to sell their first article. The writing will speak for itself.

Publishing Houses

The world of publishing is a busy and exciting place, filled with risks and surprises and, sometimes, disappointments. Without the publishing world, writers would never see their words in print; there would be no magazines, newspapers, or books for the public to enjoy, no textbooks for students and teachers to work with, no written sources for information on any subject.

Those in the publishing industry wield a great deal of power. They determine what books and stories will see print and, to some extent, help to shape the tastes of the reading public.

It's a competitive business, with financial concerns often determining which books will get published. Editors and agents have to be able to recognize good writing and know what topics are popular and what will sell.

For editors and agents, as well as writers, there's nothing more exciting than seeing a book you worked on, whether as a writer, editor, or negotiator, to finally see print and land in the bookstores. The hope is always there that the book will take off and find its way to the bestseller list and into the homes of thousands of readers. Then everyone is happy, from bookstore owners to the sales team and distributors.

But there are only ten to fifteen slots on the various bestseller lists, and with thousands of books published each year, the odds are against producing a "blockbuster."

Although some books have steady sales and can stay on the publisher's backlist for years, others don't do as well and can disappear from bookstore shelves after only a month or so.

Every book is a gamble; no one can ever predict what will happen. But successful editors and agents thrive on the excitement. In the publishing world, anything is possible.

How Publishing Houses Are Structured

A small press that puts out only three or four books a year might operate with a staff of only two or three. Each person has to wear many hats: as acquisitions editor, finding new projects to publish; as typesetter and proofreader; as sales manager; as promoter and publicist; as clerk and secretary.

The large publishing houses, which for the most part are located in New York City, can have hundreds of employees and are separated into different departments such as editorial, contracts, legal, sales and marketing, and publicity and promotion.

Within each department there are a number of different job titles. These are some of the different positions within the editorial department, although often the duties can overlap: editorial assistant, assistant/associate editor, editor, senior editor, acquisitions editor, managing editor, production editor, executive editor, editor in chief, publisher, and president.

Editors work in book-producing publishing houses or for magazines and newspapers. Editors read manuscripts, talk with writers, and decide which books or stories and articles they will publish. Editors also have to read what other houses or publications are printing to know what's out there and what's selling.

Once a manuscript is selected for publication, an editor oversees the various steps to produce the finished product, from line editing for mistakes to the book or magazine cover art and copy. Editors also regularly attend editorial meetings and occasionally travel to writers' conferences to speak to aspiring writers and to find new talent.

Training and Qualifications

Most editors have at least a bachelor's degree in communications, English, journalism, or any relevant liberal arts or humanities major. It is helpful to also be familiar with publishing law and contracts and to know how to type or word process.

In publishing it's rare for someone to start out as an editor without any prior experience. Within a publishing house there is a distinct ladder most editors climb as they gain experience and develop a successful track record. They usually start out as editorial assistants, answering the phone, opening and distributing the mail, and typing correspondence. Some editorial assistants are first readers for their editors; they'll read a manuscript, then write a reader's report. If it's a good report, the editor will take a look at the manuscript.

Most editorial assistants learn the editing process from the editor they work for, and over time move up into editorial positions with more and more responsibility.

Salaries

Editors are generally paid a set salary. Although their salary is not dependent week to week on the sales success of the books they choose to publish, an editor with a good track record is likely to be promoted and given raises. Starting pay, however, is not particularly glamorous.

Finding Media Jobs

Get a Foot in the Door

In the world of newspapers, magazines, and book publishing, some experts advise taking any job you can to get your foot in the door. If you wanted to be an editor, for example, you could start out as a contract assistant, then move into an editorial position and up the ladder to senior editor or higher. If you get yourself in the door and get to know the people in the department for which you prefer to work, your chances are better than an unknown candidate wanting to go immediately into an editorial position.

Internships

Another successful method is to take more than the one required college internship. If you can get involved in two or even three internships, you'll make more contacts and have a better chance of lining up full-time employment when you graduate. At the same time you'll be adding to your portfolio and creating impressive specifics to include on your resume.

For help in locating media employers, turn to Appendix C, where you will find a listing of directories, magazines, and other resource books.

What It's Really Like

Meet Rod Stafford Hagwood, Newspaper Fashion Editor

Rod Stafford Hagwood earned his bachelor's degree in broadcast journalism with a minor in English from Memphis State University. He started freelance writing in college and in 1990 moved directly from an internship into his present job as fashion editor at the *Sun-Sentinel* in Fort Lauderdale, Florida.

Rod Stafford Hagwood's Background

"It was not any great career plan. My guidance counselor in high school suggested I consider law, maybe because my father was an attorney, but that really didn't interest me. There were so many rules. I needed to do something where I wasn't strapped in. I was interested in writing, though I didn't really know what to do to make a living out of it.

"I started freelancing for local papers while I was in college, writing entertainment. I got lucky and met a lot of people who helped arrange interviews for me with people I normally wouldn't have been able to get. For example, I got to interview Tom Cruise right before *Top Gun* came out, and Emilio Estevez and Molly Ringwald. I met George Michael at the premiere of *Pretty in Pink*. We sat down on the stairs and I interviewed him.

"By the time I graduated, for someone who didn't have a plan, I already had published interviews with all these people, an impressive portfolio, and a job offer with Gannett, which is the parent company of a lot of newspapers, including *USA Today*. They said I could intern at one of their papers and that I'd have a full-time job when I finished.

"I interned at the *Arkansas Gazette*. Again, fate put me in the right place. While getting involved in fund-raisers in Little Rock, I got to meet Mr. and Mrs. Clinton. I wrote about them constantly. I got to write about everything. I reviewed classical music, wrote about fashion and society pieces. I did everything from flying with the Blue Angels to attending debutante balls in restricted country clubs.

"Even though I already had a firm offer with Gannett, I wasn't sure for what paper I wanted to work. Then the fashion editor of *USA Today* told me about an opening at the paper she used to work for, in Fort Lauderdale, Florida. The job was as fashion editor.

"I knew one person in Ft. Lauderdale and he had a boat. To be honest, I was more interested in getting to spend a weekend in Florida than I was in the interview—I had already been offered a job. I was happy and feeling very secure. Going for the free trip seemed like a fun idea.

"At the interview they wanted to hear my ideas about what I would do as the fashion editor. Because I hadn't taken the job offer very seriously, I hadn't thought of any plans. So I told them the kind of section I would want to write no matter where I was. I wanted it to be very funny, something that was whimsical and didn't take itself seriously. I wanted it to be a little naughty, too— nothing truly offensive, but just so people would say, 'Oh, there he goes again, doing that stuff.'

"And I wanted the fashion page to have a distinctive voice so that people would know instantly I had written it. They responded well to my answer and made me a very pleasant offer.

"What finally helped me make the decision to take the job was a fashion editor who worked for Reuters. This was about seven years ago, and at that time, she said to me, 'That area is it, that's next. Whatever is going to happen in fashion is going to happen in South Florida, in South Beach.'

"I took her advice and here I am. As soon as I arrived, South Beach exploded onto the world stage, and I moved straight from an internship right into an editor's job."

On the Job

"My main duty is to produce the fashion page, which comes out weekly on Sundays. That means making sure the art is up to the art department's standards, making sure the photography is up to the photography department's standards, and making sure the layout artist gets all the different elements in plenty of time so she can make them fit.

"Then there's the writing. I have to make sure the articles are written, which involves phone calls and research. It doesn't just come tripping off the tongue as people think.

"I cover trends. I'm not going to do a story on Naomi Campbell or Veronica Webb just because they're famous models. But this season, for example, we saw a lot of Asian models on the runway. That's the start of a trend and I'll do a story on that. But I don't cover fads. By the time a fad got in the paper it would be over.

The Upsides of the Job

"The ability to define my own rules. If I'm interested in something, I can go find out about it. It's the only job I know where I can tell my boss I'm heading out to the mall and that's perfectly acceptable. Last week I went to the beach. I got an item for my column out of it, but the point is I told my editor, 'I'm going to the beach to see what people are wearing when they step off the sand,' and she didn't even bat an eye. That's the fun part of the job. If something catches your eye, you can go investigate it.

"Another example is that large, full-service, upscale salons have started producing their own hair products on private labels. I spent four days last week in hair salons being pampered and asking questions like, 'What do you know about chemistry?' or 'What makes you able to produce these products?' This is a wonderful kind of freedom and it keeps you from becoming jaded and tired in your job. You'll never be bored."

Advice from Rod Stafford Hagwood

"You have to be secure with yourself to be in this business. There are so many extremely insecure and difficult people in the fashion industry. I would have made a wonderful ambassador; you spend a lot of time trying to charm temperamental people.

"I think my parents taught me a wonderful lesson: You have to be the one to define who and what you are; don't let anyone else define you. Being black and being a male, and a fashion editor, you have to be secure. And if you have that kind of security, you are always in control and you won't get upset by what other people do."

CHAPTER TEN

Event Planners

Have you ever attended a large wedding, a corporate function, an educational seminar, or a city festival—and wondered what went on behind the scenes to create such a well-coordinated event? Perhaps you already have a good idea. If so, you might see how a career as an event planner is ideally suited to your eye-to-detail personality. Careful attention to the details makes events successful.

Any bride knows what's involved in pulling off a topnotch wedding. Just look at some of the details:

Setting a date

Obtaining the necessary licenses

Arranging financing

Reserving the location for the wedding ceremony

Reserving the location for the reception

Engaging the services of the person to perform the ceremony

Choosing a menu

Choosing or arranging for china and silverware

For an outdoor event—ordering tables, cloths, tents, etc.

Ordering flowers and coordinating their delivery

Designing and printing napkins or matchbooks

Hiring musicians

Choosing bridesmaids, ushers, the best man, the flower girl, the ring bearer

Ordering the cake and its centerpiece

Creating an invitation list

Designing and ordering invitations

Addressing, stamping, and mailing invitations

Arranging for transportation and/or accommodation for out of town guests

Arranging for transportation to the wedding ceremony and reception

There's probably more—and don't forget the honeymoon and all the travel plans that involves.

A seminar or corporate event will have many of the same details to attend to—and often more than one person will work to bring all the elements together. A bride, for example, would have the help of her mother or sisters or friends—or perhaps she'd hire a wedding planner. And that's where you'd come in.

What It's Really Like

The vast majority of event planners are self-employed. Others work for hotels, the local government body or corporation holding the event, or for businesses that specialize in this particular kind of service. Let's meet a successful event planner and learn from her.

Meet Mary Tribble, Event Planner

Mary Tribble is the president and owner of Mary Tribble Creations, an event planning and production company located in

Charlotte, North Carolina. In 1982 she earned her B.A. in art history from Wake Forest University in Winston-Salem, North Carolina. She is one of forty people in the country to have earned the Certified Special Event Professional (CSEP) designation from the International Special Event Society (ISES). She has also attended countless continuing education courses through industry conventions. And she is also asked frequently to speak on event planning at regional and national conventions.

Mary Tribble's Background

"I was working at an advertising agency as an account executive when one of my clients asked the agency to plan a grand opening event for their new offices. As a special project, it ended up being my responsibility. It was a huge event—a black-tie gala with a laser light show—and I loved every minute of the planning. I knew I wanted to be involved in events from that time on. At first, we opened a small division at the agency for event planning, but I soon went out on my own. I was twenty-four at the time.

"I started with nothing more than a Rolodex, sitting on my bed in my apartment. No computer, nothing. I got a loan from a friendly investor for $5,000, which tided me over until the checks started coming in. That was eleven years ago.

"After about two years in business, I rented a small office, then hired my first person, who is still with me. I now have three employees, which is a gracious plenty as far as I'm concerned.

"Now that the industry has gotten so much more sophisticated, I'm not sure I'd be able to get by the way I did back then. Clients want event planners who are educated in their industry, carry all the proper insurance—and all that takes money. I have very nice offices in downtown Charlotte, and I think that adds credibility to my company.

"Now, because I've been around so long, I get a lot of my business through word-of-mouth—but I still have to market my services. That's usually through phone calls and sending out my brochure to prospects. I don't do much advertising—not even in the Yellow Pages. But I'm very active in the Chamber of Commerce and am a member of our Convention and Visitors bureau and the International Special Events Society. A lot of business comes through networking with those groups."

On the Job

"It's crazy, stress-filled, but fun. The other day would be a good example of a typical day:

7:30 A.M.—meeting with a client about a huge event we're planning for the millennium.

9:00 A.M.—back to the office, re-worked a budget for a wedding client we have. (The mother wanted it ALL, but the father had called me into his office—without his wife—to tell me what he was willing to spend.)

10:30 A.M.—Meeting with a client about another event.

12 noon—Off to exercise, then lunch at desk.

1:00 P.M.—Sales calls during the first part of the afternoon.

2:30 P.M.—Brainstorming meeting with staff. Interrupted by call from a client to put together an event in a week. Reconvened staff to brainstorm again.

4:00 P.M.—Worked on writing up a proposal.

5:30 P.M.—Visited a potential rehearsal dinner site.

6:30 P.M.—Home

"My days are rarely, if ever, relaxed. A typical day has three to six meetings, plus phone calls, deadlines for proposals, budgeting, worrying about payroll, dealing with employees' problems, making sales calls, doing diagrams of event layouts, trudging around construction sites, meeting with vendors and clients, fielding phone calls from people who want to pick my brain about the event biz, etc.

"The work atmosphere is usually what I'd described as 'frantic fun.' I try to run a flexible company with a sense of humor—practical jokes are encouraged—but I expect everyone to roll up their sleeves and get the job done.

"In the busy season, I work sixty to sixty-five hours a week. When it's less busy, about fifty. My employees work about forty-five to fifty hours, since they only work events they are assigned (I'm usually at them all).

"Weddings can be especially difficult to plan because there are so many personalities involved. With a corporate client, I'm usually answering to one person, and that person has usually reached a consensus with their staff as to what the event should be. With a wedding, the bride, the MOB (Mother of the Bride), the FOB (Father of the Bride), the in-laws, and the groom all have different expectations.

"The bride—and the MOB—have been dreaming of this day for twenty-some years, so their expectations are very high. The FOB is usually worried about what the costs will be and can't understand why the MOB wants to spend $2,000 on place card holders. There have been times when MOB, bride, and FOB are diametrically opposed, and I've had to step into some very tense situations, acting as mediator. It can be a very emotional experience for all concerned, and it's my job to stay calm and bring everyone to a consensus.

"It's also my job to exceed the twenty-some years of expectations—create a fairy tale wedding that the bride will remember forever—whatever her style or taste. One month that might mean a casual lakeside wedding with a rustic wedding canopy covered with lavender, roses, and vines. The next it could be a glittering gold wedding patterned after Versailles in a hotel ballroom, with huge gold candelabra centerpieces.

"That particular glittering gold wedding was something I had only three and half weeks to plan—and it was for five hundred people! The groom's mother was ill, and the wedding had been set for six months off. But all were concerned that she might not make it. So, BAM! We had to plan a huge gala in less than a month—in a different hotel than had been originally reserved.

"In addition to weddings, I plan just about any kind of corporate event—grand openings, client celebrations, incentive events, employee receptions, etc. This could be anything from an outdoor laser light show for twenty-five thousand people to a elegant cocktail party to a stage show production. We come up with the ideas, then plan the whole thing from start to finish—invitations, catering, decorating, special effects, entertainment, etc. We contract all of that out, though. We don't keep lasers in stock!

"Paying attention to the details is the most important part of event planning. We can come up with all the wonderful themes in the world, but if we don't interpret them with details, they mean nothing. When we plan an event, everything—invitations, decorations, entertainment, place cards, gifts, signage—is selected to enhance the concept of the event.

"Also, the day-to-day planning is very detail oriented. We have to imagine an event from the time someone gets the invitation to how they will get there, where they will park, who will greet them, how the event will begin, and how it will end.

"For every event, we create a schedule for setup, which is an hour-by-hour outline of everything that will happen leading up to the event. Sometimes, if it's a complicated event, that document can be ten to twelve pages long.

"We also create a show schedule that outlines the event itself. Say, for instance, we are producing an awards ceremony. We'll develop a show schedule (this one's minute-by-minute!) that tells what person goes to the stage at what time, what they'll do or say on stage, how the lights in the house will be set, how the lights on the stage might change, what the audience is seeing on the video screen, etc. Show schedules have to be incredibly detailed so that there's no downtime on stage.

"What I like most about my work is the satisfaction that I've surpassed the client's dreams and expectations. The gasp factor. Also, I like the diversity—no day is ever the same, and I do get to spend a good deal of my time with creative people, brainstorming new ideas and coming up with new challenges.

"I also get a rush from the stress the events create. I like to problem-solve on my toes and come up with quick and innovative solutions.

"The long hours are a downside, though. It's not too uncommon for us to work eighteen to twenty hours with no break, and I'm getting too old for that! I work a lot of weekends and evenings. Other downsides are dealing with all the details of the event—which is why I have employees. I like to conceptualize the event, but the drudgery of all the phone calls and meetings on minute things can be tiresome.

Advice from Mary Tribble

"Education, education, education! Just because you planned your sorority rush parties doesn't mean you can plan events professionally. We take on a great deal of responsibility when we put a thousand people in a hotel ballroom. Is the event safe? Does our layout meet fire codes? Are our linens, draping, candles approved by the fire department? Is the event handicapped accessible? Does the caterer meet health code requirements? Do we have enough liability insurance?

"You have to think about workers' comp and if we have permission to record and/or play licensed music. Are we following union regulations? Will the electricity carry the load of the equipment we've brought in?

"Planning events is not all fun and games, and you must make sure you're providing your client with a safe and secure event. You need to stay on the cutting edge trends and make sure your clients are getting the best services possible.

"The International Special Events Society has chapters all over the world, most of which offer monthly educational meetings. George Washington University now offers a degree in Events Management. *Special Events Magazine* hosts an annual convention for three thousand event producers, with great education sessions. There are plenty of avenues now for you to get the education that even I didn't have when I started out.

"Even if you don't go for a specific event planning degree, degrees in public relations, marketing, or hotel/hospitality management can prepare you to some degree. Public relations courses very often include sections on events.

"In addition to education, you need hands-on experience. Volunteer on a committee for a local non-profit organization's fundraiser. Intern at an event production company, hotel, or catering firm. The experience you receive will be a great investment.

"The perfect event planner personality? You need to be a left brain/right brain person—you need the creative side to come up with new and exciting ideas, but you also need the detail side to execute them. That's a tough combination.

"You also need to thrive on stress—and learn not to panic in bad situations. You need to be quick on your toes, you need to be a negotiator, and you need to have a calming influence on people. Our clients need someone calm and relaxed in the face of the controlled chaos."

Becoming ISES Certified

You must apply to ISES first to be eligible for certification. You'll receive a form outlining the "point system" to determine whether or not you can sit for the exam. You accumulate points from years in the business, attending continuing education classes, etc. Once you have enough points, you sit for a written exam.

The whole process is not that easy, but it pays off two ways: respect from your peers and your standing in the event community are raised, and you can use certification as a marketing tool for clients. Clients will usually be impressed when you tell them what the CSEP designation means.

For more information on certification, contact The International Special Events Society, listed in Appendix A.

To keep on top of what's happening in the field, you can subscribe to *Special Events Magazine* from Miramar Communications, 23815 Stuart Ranch Road, Malibu, CA 90265.

CHAPTER ELEVEN

Efficiency Experts

*E*fficiency experts (what could be a more perfect career for a perfectionist?) are also known as management analysts or management consultants. Others who use similar skills are computer systems analysts, operations research analysts, economists, and financial analysts.

A rapidly growing small company needs a better system of control over inventories and expenses. An established manufacturing company decides to relocate to another state and needs assistance planning the move. After acquiring a new division, a large company realizes that its corporate structure must be reorganized. A division chief of a government agency wants to know why the division's contracts are always going over budget.

These are just a few of the many organizational problems that management analysts, as they are called in government agencies, and management consultants, as business firms refer to them, help solve. Although their job titles may differ, their job duties are essentially the same.

The work of management analysts and consultants varies from employer to employer and from project to project. For example, some projects require several consultants to work together, each specializing in one area; at other times, they will work independently.

In general, analysts and consultants collect, review, and analyze information; make recommendations; and often assist in the implementation of their proposal.

Both public and private organizations use consultants for a variety of reasons. Some don't have the internal resources needed to handle a project; others need a consultant's expertise to determine what resources will be required or problems encountered if they pursue a particular course of action; others want to get outside advice on how to resolve organizational problems that have already been identified or to avoid troublesome problems that could arise.

Firms providing consulting services range in size from solo practitioners to large international organizations employing thousands of consultants. Some firms specialize by industry, others by type of business function, such as human resources or information systems.

Consulting services usually are provided on a contract basis. A company solicits proposals from consulting firms specializing in the area in which it needs assistance. These proposals include the estimated cost and scope of the project, staffing requirements, and the deadline. The company then selects the proposal that best meets its needs.

Upon getting an assignment or contract, consultants define the nature and extent of the problem. During this phase of the job, they may analyze data such as annual revenues, employment, or expenditures; interview employees; or observe the operations of the organizational unit.

Next, they use their knowledge of management systems and their expertise in a particular area to develop solutions. In the course of preparing their recommendations, they must take into account the general nature of the business, the relationship the firm has with others in that industry, and the firm's internal organization, as well as information gained through data collection and analysis.

Once they have decided on a course of action, consultants usually report their findings and recommendations to the client, often in writing. In addition, they often make oral presentations regarding their findings. For some projects, this is all that is required; for others, consultants may assist in the implementation of their suggestions.

Management analysts in government agencies use the same skills as their private-sector colleagues to advise managers in government on many types of issues, most of which are similar to the problems faced by private firms. For example, if an agency is planning to purchase several personal computers, it first must determine which type to buy, given its budget and data processing needs. Management analysts would assess the various types of machines available and determine which best meets their department's needs.

Working Conditions

Management analysts and consultants usually divide their time between their offices and their client's operation. Although much of their time is spent indoors in clean, well-lighted offices, they may have to visit a client's production facility where conditions may not be so favorable. They must follow established safety procedures when making field visits to sites where they may encounter potentially hazardous conditions.

Typically, analysts and consultants work at least forty hours a week. Overtime is common, especially when deadlines loom. In addition, because they must spend a significant portion of their time with clients, they may travel frequently.

Self-employed consultants can set their workload and hours and work at home. On the other hand, their livelihood depends on their ability to maintain and expand their client base, which can be difficult at times.

Employment Opportunities

Management analysts and consultants held about 240,000 jobs in 1996. Four out of ten of these workers were self-employed. Most of the rest worked in management consulting firms and for federal, state, and local governments. The majority of those working for the federal government were found in the U.S. Department of Defense.

Management analysts and consultants are found throughout the country, but employment is concentrated in metropolitan areas.

Training and Qualifications

There are no universal educational requirements for entry-level jobs in this field. However, employers in private industry prefer to hire those with a master's degree in business administration or a discipline related to the firm's area of specialization. Those individuals hired straight out of school with only a bachelor's degree are likely to work as research associates or junior consultants, rather than full-fledged management consultants. It is possible for research associates to advance up the career ladder if they demonstrate a strong aptitude for consulting but, more often, they need to get an advanced degree to do so.

Many entrants to this occupation have, in addition to the appropriate formal education, several years of experience in management or in another occupation.

Most government agencies hire those with a bachelor's degree and no work experience as entry-level management analysts, and often provide formal classroom training in management analysis.

Many fields of study provide a suitable formal educational background for this occupation because of the diversity of problem areas addressed by management analysts and consultants. These include most areas of business and management, as well as computer and information sciences and engineering.

Management analysts and consultants who are hired directly from school sometimes participate in formal company training programs. These programs may include instruction on policies and procedures, computer systems and software, research processes, and management practices and principles. Because of their previous industry experience, most who enter at middle levels do not participate in formal company training programs. However, regardless of background, analysts and consultants routinely attend conferences to keep abreast of current developments in their field. Additionally, some large firms offer in-house formal training programs for all levels of staff.

Management analysts and consultants often work under little or no supervision, so they should be independent and self-motivated. Analytical skills, strong oral communication and written skills, good judgment, the ability to manage time well, and creativity in developing solutions to problems are other desirable qualities for prospective management analysts and consultants.

In large consulting firms, beginners usually start as a member of a consulting team. The team is responsible for the entire project and each consultant is assigned to a particular area. As consultants gain experience, they may be assigned to work on one specific project full-time, taking on more responsibility and managing their own hours. At the senior level, consultants may supervise entry-level workers and become increasingly involved in seeking out new business. Those with exceptional skills may eventually become a partner or principal in the firm. Others with entrepreneurial ambition may open their own firm.

A high percentage of management consultants are self-employed, partly because start-up costs are low. Little capital is required initially, and it is possible for self-employed consultants to share office space, administrative help, and other resources with other self-employed consultants or small consulting firms, thus reducing overhead costs.

The Institute of Management Consultants (a division of the Council of Consulting Organizations) offers the Certified Management Consultant (CMC) designation to those who pass an examination and meet minimum levels of education and experience. Certification is not mandatory for management consultants to practice, but it may give a job seeker a competitive advantage.

Salaries

Salaries for management analysts and consultants vary widely by experience, education, and employer. In 1996, those who were wage and salary workers had median annual earnings of about $46,000.

In 1994, according to the Association of Management Consulting Firms (ACME), earnings including bonuses and/or profit sharing for research associates in ACME member firms averaged $30,3400; for entry level consultants, $41,800; for management consultants, $58,300; for senior consultants, $89,200; for junior partners, $120,100; and for senior partners, $194,000.

Typical benefits for salaried analysts and consultants include health and life insurance, a retirement plan, vacation and sick leave, profit sharing, and bonuses for outstanding work.

In addition, all travel expenses usually are reimbursed by their employer. Self-employed consultants usually have to maintain an office and do not receive employer-provided benefits.

What It's Really Like

Meet Moana Re, Efficiency Expert/Analyst

Moana Re worked for three years for a management consulting firm in Dallas, Texas. She attended both the University of Miami and the University of Colorado and earned her B.A. in education from the latter.

Moana Re's Background

"I was a researcher/analyst, or what some people call an 'efficiency expert,' for a major consulting group for three years. A consulting group is a body with experience and expertise based upon years in the business world who, for a price, offers its advice and services to companies. These companies basically want to improve their customer service and bottom-dollar line. All different kinds of companies contract with us—and large ones, too, such as JC Penney and Compaq Computer.

"Primarily, my job was to discover how a business process or call flow was working—or not working. A business process is the steps a business takes—from answering the phone or opening the door to making a sale and documenting that sale. It is a map of how a business works.

"A call flow is a diagram that shows what occurs when a phone call is answered, and what decisions must be made to logically follow the call and assist the customer. You can liken it to calling your bank. First the call is automatically answered, then you are given choices; when you make that choice you may be given yet another choice.

"When we were about to bid for a job, I would dig up all kinds of information about the company and the services they currently offer, as well as what areas they may be having problems in, the size of the company, any financial information, and of course, who the principle players are.

"To do this I would interview employees and key management people. You'd be surprised what a gap that can be. Management tells me they are following current processes much as they may appear in a manual—but the employees describe a whole different scenario.

"In these interviews, I would try to find out what the current job is like for the people I talk to and what they perceive will help them and the company. I would also inventory their equipment.

"I took the information I gathered, along with notes from meetings with top management regarding what they envisioned the company to be doing, and I translated that information into a flowchart I drew up. The flowchart visibly shows how the steps are working or not.

"I would present that chart to my bosses and they would discuss (along with others in the field) how best this flow should work to enrich the profits and business for the company.

"This often takes some rather keen deductive reasoning based on business processes that are currently being considered or are, in fact, already in place. I then would generate a report to my bosses, who discussed what I discerned.

"They would either agree with me, or they'd ask me to adjust some of the processes I proposed. Once we all agreed on the new process flow, I drew a new business process flow diagram and we took it to the customer, who then made the decisions on whether or not they were willing to implement my recommendations.

"If they did not agree—sometimes, even though their practices may have been adopted by the 'seat of their pants,' they would be unwilling to let them go. Then we began that part of the process all over again.

"If collectively we'd see that by changing their current process, it would improve their objective, they generally asked for statistics, which I begin to gather from other sources, such as other companies or analysts I'd talk to.

"If they agreed with my analysis, it would get rubber stamped by all departments. I'd begin a new set of process flows to be distributed throughout their system.

"The work could be rather tedious in that I couldn't miss a step. When I did interviews and then showed my flowchart to the customer, quite often they'd then remember other steps that they did not mention previously. It is amazing to see what you do spread out on paper. It sharpens your focus on exactly what you are doing.

"My job could be very intense. It began when the proposal is sold to the client. It's at that point that I was sent onsite to review what the business flow and call flows are currently. This may take quite a bit of time, if it is a large company. After each interview session, I'd develop flow charts. When I completed an area of business or a department, then I'd analyze the results and compare it to the proposed result that we hoped to initiate. Sometimes this takes digging into the company practices even further and can lead to interviews with the principles.

"I also delved into what other companies of similar experience have done. I search to see what the future trends are and then begin to make new flow charts with proposed changes.

"I worked nine to five usually, unless I was with a client and then it could be anywhere, anytime. About 30 percent of my job I spent traveling, too. It depends. Some of our clients' contracts are short-term and they want us to work only on a particular area of concern (such as call centers) or it may be longer—I just finished a one-year job. The more work you do for a company, the more traveling back and forth you do.

"On the other side of my job, I also wrote the proposals, brochures, and news releases and I was the final wordsmith for all outgoing correspondence that went to the client."

Advice from Moana Re

"It is my opinion that a person who is investigative by nature, thorough, and enjoys people would do well in a job such as this. The advice I might give is to be as flexible as possible and go with the flow."

Professional Associations

F or more information on the careers covered in this book, contact the appropriate professional associations listed below.

Chapter Two

Accountants and Auditors

Information about different accounting licenses and the standards for licensure in your state may be obtained from your state board of accountancy. A list of the addresses and chief executives of all state boards of accountancy is available from:

National Association of State Boards of Accountancy
380 Lexington Avenue, Suite 200
New York, NY 10168-0002

Information about careers in certified public accounting and about CPA standards and examinations may be obtained from:

American Institute of Certified Public Accountants
1211 Avenue of the Americas
New York, NY 10036-8775

Information on management and other specialized fields of accounting and auditing and on the Certified Management Accountant program is available from:

Institute of Management Accountants
10 Paragon Drive
Montvale, NJ 07645-1760

National Society of Public Accountants and the Accreditation
  Council for Accountancy and Taxation
1010 North Fairfax Street
Alexandria, VA 22314

The Institute of Internal Auditors
249 Maitland Avenue
Altamonte Springs, FL 32701-4201

The EDP Auditors Association
455 Kehoe Boulevard, Suite 106
Carol Stream, IL 60188-0180

For information on accredited accounting programs and educational institutions offering a specialization in accounting or business management, contact:

American Assembly of Collegiate Schools of Business
605 Old Ballas Road, Suite 220
St. Louis, MO 63141

Actuaries

For facts about actuarial careers, contact:

American Academy of Actuaries
1720 I Street NW, Seventh Floor
Washington, DC 20006

For information about actuarial careers in life and health insurance, contact:

Society of Actuaries
475 North Martingale Road, Suite 800
Schaumburg, IL 60173-2226

For information about actuarial careers in property and casualty insurance, contact:

Casualty Actuarial Society
1100 North Glebe Road, Suite 600
Arlington, VA 22201

Career information on actuaries specializing in pensions is available from:

American Society of Pension Actuaries
4350 North Fairfax Drive, Suite 820
Arlington, VA 22203

Statisticians

For information about career opportunities in statistics, contact:

American Statistical Association
1429 Duke Street
Alexandria, VA 22314

For information on a career as a mathematical statistician, contact:

Institute of Mathematical Statistics
3401 Investment Boulevard, No. 7
Hayward, CA 94545

Information on federal job opportunities is available from area offices of the state employment service and the U.S. Office of Personnel Management or from Federal Job Information Centers located in various large cities throughout the country.

Chapter Three

Lawyers

The American Bar Association annually publishes A *Review of Legal Education in the United States,* which provides detailed information on each of the 177 law schools approved by the ABA, state requirements for admission to legal practice, a directory of state bar examination administrators, and other information on legal education. Single copies are free from the ABA, but there is a fee for multiple copies. Free information on the bar examination, financial aid for law students, and law as a career may also be obtained from:

Member Services
American Bar Association
541 North Fairbanks Court
Chicago, IL 60611-3314

Information on the LSAT, the Law School Data Assembly Service, applying to law school, and financial aid for law students may be obtained from:

Law School Admission Services
P.O. Box 40
Newtown, PA 18940

The specific requirements for admission to the bar in a particular state or other jurisdiction may also be obtained at the state

capital, from the clerk of the Supreme Court, or the administrator of the State Board of Bar Examiners.

Chapter Four

Architects

Information about education and careers in architecture can be
obtained from:

Director, Careers in Architecture Programs
The American Institute of Architects
1735 New York Avenue NW
Washington, DC 20006

Landscape Architects

Additional information, including a list of colleges and
universities offering accredited programs in landscape architecture, is available from:

American Society of Landscape Architects
4401 Connecticut Avenue NW
Washington, DC 20008

General information on registration or licensing requirements
is available from:

Council of Landscape Architectural Registration Boards
12700 Fair Lakes Circle, Suite 110
Fairfax, VA 22033

Chapter Five

Surveyors and Mapmakers

Information about career opportunities, licensure requirements, and the survey technician certification program is available from:

American Congress on Surveying and Mapping
5410 Grosvenor Lane
Bethesda, MD 20814-2122

General information on careers in photogrammetry is available from:

American Society for Photogrammetry and Remote Sensing
5410 Grosvenor Lane, Suite 200
Bethesda, MD 20814

Chapter Six

Engineers

High school students interested in obtaining general information on a variety of engineering disciplines should contact the Junior Engineering Technical Society by sending a self-addressed business size envelope with six first-class stamps to:

JETS-Guidance
1420 King Street, Suite 405
Alexandria, VA 22314

Non-high school students and those wanting more detailed information should contact societies representing the individual branches of engineering. Each can provide information about careers in the particular branch.

American Society of Civil Engineers
345 East Forty-seventh Street
New York, NY 10017

The Society for Mining, Metallurgy, and Exploration, Inc.
P.O. Box 625002
Littleton, CO 80162-5002

For information on aerospace careers, send $3 to:

American Institute of Aeronautics and Astronautics, Inc.
AIAA Student Programs
The Aerospace Center
370 L'Enfant Promenade SW
Washington, DC 20024-2518

Other resources include the following:

Institute of Industrial Engineers, Inc.
25 Technology Park/Atlanta
Norcross, GA 30092

The Minerals, Metals, & Materials Society
420 Commonwealth Drive
Warrendale, PA 15086-7514

ASM International
Student Outreach Program
Materials Park, OH 44073

Institute of Electrical and Electronics Engineers
1828 L Street NW, Suite 1202
Washington, DC 20036

American Nuclear Society
555 North Kensington Avenue
LaGrange Park, IL 60525

The American Society of Mechanical Engineers
345 East Forty-seventh Street
New York, NY 10017

American Society of Heating, Refrigerating, and Air-
   Conditioning Engineers, Inc.
1791 Tullie Circle NE
Atlanta, GA 30329

American Institute of Chemical Engineers
345 East Forty-seventh Street
New York, NY 10017

American Chemical Society
Career Services
1155 Sixteenth Street NW
Washington, DC 20036

For information on chemical engineering technicians,
contact:

American Institute of Chemical Engineers
Attention: Mr. Chung Lam
345 East Forty-seventh Street
New York, NY 10017

Society of Petroleum Engineers
222 Palisades Creek Drive
Richardson, TX 75080

Chapter Seven

Art Conservators

American Association of Museums
1225 Eye Street NW, Suite 200
Washington, DC 20005

American Institute for Conservation of Historic and Artistic
  Works
1717 K Street NW, Suite 301
Washington, DC 20006

Archaeological Conservancy
415 Orchard Drive
Santa Fe, NM 87501

Association for Preservation Technology, International
P.O. Box 8178
Fredericksburg, VA 22404

Association of Art Museum Directors
41 East Sixty-fifth Street
New York, NY 10021

Association of College and University Museums and Galleries
c/o University Museum
Southern Illinois University at Edwardsville
Edwardsville, IL 62026-1150

Independent Curators Incorporated
799 Broadway, Suite 205
New York, NY 10003

Internship Program, Office of Museum Programs
Smithsonian Institution
Arts & Industries Building, Room 2235
Washington, DC 20560

International Association of Museum Facility Administrators
P.O. Box 1505
Washington, DC 20013-1505

International Institute for Conservation–
  Canadian Group (IIC-CG)
P.O. Box 9195
Ottawa, Ontario K1G 3T9
Canada

Chapter Eight

Researchers

Board for Certification of Genealogists
P.O. Box 5816
Falmouth, VA 22403-5816

Genealogical Library
Church of Jesus Christ of Latter-Day Saints
Family History Library
35 North West Temple
Salt Lake City, UT 84150

National Genealogical Society
4527 Seventeenth Street North
Arlington, VA 22207-2399

Chapter Nine

Writers and Editors

American Newspaper Publishers Association
The Newspaper Center
11600 Sunrise Valley Drive
Reston, VA 22091

American Society of Journalists and Authors
1501 Broadway, Suite 302
New York, NY 10036

American Society of Magazine Editors
919 Third Avenue
New York, NY 10022

American Society of Media Photographers
14 Washington Road, Suite 502
Princeton Junction, NJ 08550

American Society of Newspaper Editors
P.O. Box 4090
Reston, VA 22090-1700

Associated Press Broadcasters Association
1825 K Street NW, Suite 710
Washington, DC 20006

Association of American Publishers
71 Fifth Avenue
New York, NY 10010

Association of Authors Representatives (AAR)
10 Astor Place, Third Floor
New York, NY 10003

Author's League of America
330 West Forty-second Street, Twenty-ninth Floor
New York, NY 10036

Broadcast Education Association
1771 N Street NW
Washington, DC 20036

The Dow Jones Newspaper Fund
P.O. Box 300
Princeton, NJ 08543-0300

Investigative Reporters and Editors
100 Neff Hall
University of Missouri
Columbia, MO 65211

Magazine Publishers Association
919 Third Avenue, Twenty-second Floor
New York, NY 10022

National Association of Publisher Representatives
399 East Seventy-second Street, Suite 3F
New York, NY 10021

National Conference of Editorial Writers
6223 Executive Boulevard
Rockville, MD 20852

National Newspaper Association
1525 Wilson Boulevard
Arlington, VA 22209

The Newspaper Guild
8611 Second Avenue
Silver Springs, MD 20910

Producers Guild of America
400 South Beverly Drive, Room 211
Beverly Hills, CA 90212

Society of National Association Publications
1150 Connecticut Avenue NW, Suite 1050
Washington, DC 20036

Chapter Ten

Event Planners
The International Special Events Society
9202 North Meridean Street, Suite 200
Indianapolis, IN 46260

Chapter Eleven

Efficiency Experts
Information about career opportunities in management consulting is available from:

The Association of Management Consulting Firms (ACME)
521 Fifth Avenue, Thirty-fifth Floor
New York, NY 10175-3598

For information about a career as a government management analyst, contact your state or local employment service.

Persons interested in a management analyst position in the federal government can obtain information from:

U.S. Office of Personnel Management
1900 E Street NW
Washington, DC 20415

Conservation Degree and Internship Training Programs

The following symbols designate the level of training the following conservation training programs offer:

U–Undergraduate

G–Graduate

P–Postgraduate

I–Internships

C–Courses

Art Conservation Department   G
State University College at Buffalo
230 Rockwell Hall
1300 Elmwood Avenue
Buffalo, NY 14222

Art Conservation Department UGP
University of Delaware and Henry Francis du Pont
Winterthur Museum
303 Old College
University of Delaware
Newark, DE 19716

Art Conservation Programme   G
Queens University
Kingston, Ontario K7L 3N6
Canada

Campbell Center for Historic Preservation Studies   C
203 East Seminary Street
Mt. Carroll, IL 61053

Canadian Conservation Institute GPI
Training and Information Division
Department of Communications
1030 Innes Road
Ottawa, Ontario K1A 0C8
Canada

Center for Conservation and Technical Studies   GPI
Harvard University Art Museums
32 Quincy Street
Cambridge, MA 02138

Columbia University   G
Graduate School of Architecture, Planning, & Preservation
400 Avery Hall
New York, NY 10027

Conservation Analytical Laboratory   UGPIC
Training Program, MSC
Smithsonian Institution
Washington, DC 20560

Conservation Center, Institute of Fine Arts G
New York University
14 East Seventy-eighth Street
New York, NY 10021

Johns Hopkins University   P
  (Ph.D. in materials science with a concentration in
  conservation science, sponsored by the Smithsonian
  Conservation Analytical Laboratory)
Department of Materials Science & Engineering
Room 102, Maryland Building
Johns Hopkins University
Baltimore, MD 21218

Getty Conservation Institute   C
4503 Glencoe Avenue
Marina del Ray, CA 90292

Rocky Mountain Conservation Center/University of Denver   C
  (Preconservation aide program and a certificate in
  preconservation studies)
2420 South University Boulevard
Denver, CO 80208

University of Pennsylvania   G
Graduate Program in Historic Preservation
Architectural Conservation Laboratory
115 Meyerson Hall
Philadelphia, PA 19104-6311

University of Texas at Austin   G
Graduate School of Library & Information Science
Preservation & Conservation Education Programs for Libraries
  and Archives
Austin, TX 78712-1276

Media Job Hunting Resources

T he following listings, directories, magazines, and resource books can help you in your job search. Most are available in the reference section of your library.

America's Largest Newspapers
14 Hickory Avenue
Takoma Park, MD 20912
  A computer listing of the names and addresses of two
  thousand editors at newspapers around the country.

Broadcasting and Cable Marketplace
R.R. Bowker
121 Chanlon Road
New Providence, NJ 07974

Encyclopedia of Associations
Gale Research, Inc.
P.O. Box 33477
Detroit, MI 48232

Gale Directory of Publications and Broadcast Media
Gale Research, Inc.
P.O. Box 33477
Detroit, MI 48232-5477

Guide to Literary Agents & Art/Photo Reps
Photographer's Market
Writer's Market
Writer's Digest Books
F & W Publications
1507 Dana Avenue
Cincinnati, OH 45207

The Literary Marketplace
R.R. Bowker
121 Chanlon Road
New Providence, NJ 07974

National Public Radio
2025 M Street, NW
Washington, DC 20036

Publishers Weekly
P.O. Box 1979
Marion, OH 43306

Writer's Digest Magazine
Writer's Digest Books
1507 Dana Avenue
Cincinnati, OH 45207

The following annual publications list all the print and broad-cast media organizations in the country and include the names and titles of primary managers and editors.

Newspapers Career Directories
National Directory of Weekly Newspapers
Editor & Publisher Yearbook
Broadcasting Yearbook

About the Author

A full-time writer of career books, Blythe Camenson works hard to help job seekers make educated choices. She firmly believes that with enough information, readers can find long-term, satisfying careers. To that end, she researches traditional as well as unusual occupations, talking to a variety of professionals about what their jobs are really like. In all of her books she includes firsthand accounts from people who reveal what to expect in each occupation.

Camenson was educated in Boston, earning her B.A. in English and psychology from the University of Massachusetts and her M.Ed. in counseling from Northeastern University.

In addition to *Careers for Perfectionists*, she has written more than two dozen books for NTC/Contemporary Publishing.